From Patricia Sperry

"School Ain't No Way..."/ Appalachian Consciousness

Ron Iannone

McCLAIN PRINTING COMPANY
PARSONS, WEST VIRGINIA 26287

1972

Standard Book Number 87012-135-9
Library of Congress Card Number 72-89122
Printed in the United States of America
Copyright © 1972 by Ronald V. Iannone
Morgantown, West Virginia
All Rights Reserved

To the children of Appalachia who helped me open my eyes and heart to their land and culture.

Table of Contents

I. Introduction 1

II. "School Ain't No Way..."/
   Appalachian Consciousness 9

III. Consuming, Schooling, and Babbling 81

IV. Appalachian Consciousness of the
    Apocalypse 105

> *If a man does not keep pace with his companions, perhaps it is because he hears a different drummer. Let him step to the music which he hears, however measured or far away.*
>
> Henry David Thoreau

****

I. Introduction

"Hello, Ron?

"It's all over, they don't want you and your program unless you can keep the kids locked up for three and a half hours. I really tried, Ron, but they couldn't accept the goals of the program. There is very little hope for us."

"Thanks Betty. I know you tried very hard. Bye."

How do you explain to someone the death of something that only lasted eleven weeks? How do you explain to someone that you have been destroyed by something that is one dimensional and rejects all alternatives? How do you explain to someone the pissed-off feeling you have when you have been jilted from a beautiful love affair? How do you explain to someone that this love affair consisted of reaching out to children who were noncommunicative and who constantly rejected your love? How do you explain to someone that your dreams of changing the system have been shattered and you don't care about reaching for the stars anymore?

Metaphorically speaking, the only similarity between this love story and Erich Segal's love story is on two dimensions; one is the questions figuratively posed above, and the other is both loves were destroyed by a terminal disease.

This story will attempt to answer some of the questions raised above. The area in which this story unfolds is the northern Appalachian area of West Virginia. At one time, this region of flat-topped ridges and steep-walled valleys was highly endowed with dense forests, abundant game, and thick veins of coal. In some few parts of this region, it is still as virgin as it was when the first settlers came seeking a new freedom. Today, much of this beautiful area has been spoiled. The rivers are polluted with trash, coal residues, and garbage. Along the highways one sees at times only abandoned cars and houses with tin-can litter and trash scattered around the cars and houses. Many of the beautiful forests which were covered with white oak, pine, and walnut have been destroyed by either strip-mining or highway construction. It is interesting to note that as much of this beautiful land has been spoiled, so have the people in this region. The first settlers that came into this area were seeking a freedom with very few constraints. They were not concerned with being a British colony or setting up a religious community as was being done by the settlers on the eastern coast. Using the vernacular of today's youth, the first settlers in northern Appalachia wanted to "do their thing" with very little interference from the outside. They sought to live off the land by hunting and fishing and to have sort of a Thoreau-type existence. They wanted a life free from rules and regulations and a system that gave equal status to all, and in many respects they recognized no authority other than their own. Their environment helped make this possible because of the difficulty to travel into these areas; and hence, the area itself became a labyrinth repelling most outside influences for two hundred years.

This type of mountaineer and his individualistic nature of the early folk songs and poems have vanished, in many respects, from the face of the earth. The environment which he loved so much has been exploited by so-called "progress." Not only was his land raped by coal and lumber companies, but his soul was also raped. He lost out in our very highly competitive, industrial, and complex society. How this was achieved is spelled out in very cogent terms by Harry Caudill in his book *Night Comes to the Cumberland*,[*] and the rest is history. Thus, today the mountaineer is fighting for his life and culture before he loses it to the twentieth century materialism that presently engulfs the rest of the country. The mountaineer has a problem of survival.

With this bit of history of the Appalachian, I will turn my attention to the public school system in which my story took place. The public school system in this area consists of schools that date back to 1901 and the local school system is typical of many of the school systems in West Virginia. The local board of education runs the schools with a superintendent who supposedly implements their policy. The teachers are usually very dedicated, but because of miseducation, they perpetuate the closeness of people in this area. This closeness is also

[*]Harry M. Caudill, *Night Comes to the Cumberland* (Boston: Little, Brown and Company, 1962).

perpetuated by the nepotism that exists in the area. If a teacher supports the local school board policies he is rewarded; however, as a teacher, if you disagree with the policies of the school system, you may end up teaching in a school up the farthest hollow in the county school district.

The superintendent in this area has been beaten down so much by the ultraconservatism in the community and in his staff, that now he spends most of his time making sure that schools, because of their antiquated and dilapidated conditions, won't fall down on the children. He also has to contend with a powerful landlord who controls the board and the people in the rural areas of the community. The people in the rural area like this landlord because they feel he's the only one who cares about them, and that schools should be only for reading, writing, and arithmetic. Even though the Appalachians want a good education for their children, they do not know the procedure and are naive to the kind of effort it requires. Yet, many Appalachian youth still consider the object of education to be "getting to sixteen years old so you can quit." Many times schools are perceived as a place where one meets his future husband or wife. It is perceived as one of the few places where a young boy has a chance to court a girl because their homes are usually scattered and there is very little opportunity except at schools for boys and girls to meet. Usually if a girl is able to get engaged by sixteen, she is looked upon with envy by her girl friends.

Many more values in Appalachia concerning schools and education will become evident as my story unfolds. My story begins with receiving permission by the public school officials to attempt to develop a new alternative to education. The public school people had surmised from my writings, speeches, and articles that I was dissatisfied with the schooling process both as an educator and as a professor of teacher education. Seven different schools were approached with the idea that I was seeking some space in a school building and some pupils in order to develop and implement an alternative learning environment for both the prospective teachers and the children of Appalachia. One principal of a junior high school accepted the program while the others felt it might disrupt the order of their "smoothly running ship," as one principal put it.

As I later found out, even though this principal accepted the idea, he really didn't understand the reasoning behind its inception, but was only looking for something that might save his job, which was in jeopardy. I felt this might be good, for the less he knew, the better off I would be in developing an alternative learning environment. I was soon to find out that this was erroneous thinking on my part. The principal agreed to give me three rooms for my project. One was an industrial arts room, another was a small counseling room, and the last was a Boiler Room where walls had been put up to separate the space from a thoroughfare.

I asked for five volunteers from our population of prospective secondary teachers. The five volunteers were: a girl named Jane whose field was art and who was brought up in one of the cosmopolitan areas of West Virginia; another was Jack, a Vietnam War veteran from New Jersey, whose field was science; another was Bill, a former Peace Corps member, whose field was English and who was from a small rural area in West Virginia; and the other two were Ben and Jerry, who also were from rural West Virginia backgrounds, and were in the fields of physical education and mathematics, in that order.

The principal and his staff decided that the children in the program would be those who were disrupting the school's order. These children were for the most part from families of a working-class culture. Jack Weller uses this terminology in his discussion of the Appalachian people which was originally developed by Gans. Gans suggests that the working-class culture fits in between the lower class and the lower-middle class which exist in the northern sites such as the north and south ends in Boston, the steel-working sections in Detroit, and the ethnic sections of New York.*

The majority of the children chosen for this project came from a hollow or small valley which at one time supplied workers for a nearby mine which closed down a few years ago. There was a school near this hollow; however, it was also closed down when the county decided to centralize the school district. The children of the project usually lived in a faraway hollow buried deep in the hills with only three to five houses in it. During the winter and spring months, these hollows were sometimes inaccessible to cars and buses. Many of the children's homes consisted of three or four rooms, one was used as a kitchen, one was used as living room and a bedroom at night, and the other two rooms were usually a bedroom or bathroom. In many cases, the outdoor toilet facilities are still prevalent within these hol-

*Jack Weller, *Yesterday's People* (Lexington: University of Kentucky Press, 1966), p. 5.

lows. Their heat consisted of either a coal stove sitting in the middle of the living room or an oil furnace.

The principal felt it would be unwise to get the parents of these children involved, and in so many words, I was told if I wanted the program there at that school to "stay away from the parents."

The teachers and I were given a week to prepare for the children. We spent our time trying to get to know each other better, while also collecting materials and data on the students. As it turned out, I don't believe we could have ever been prepared for what was going to happen to us during the next eleven weeks. This is where my story begins and it will be told by revealing a large portion of the personal diary I kept during the program's tenure.

> *We all still have subject and object*
> *self and other, man and god.*
> *We have a religion of separation*
> *a preoccupation with forms*
> *which distinguish surfaces.*
>
> *To stretch the action of attention*
> *to envelop subject and object*
> *in one consciousness is learning.*
>
> (Big Rock Candy Mountain)

****

II. "School Ain't No Way..."/ Appalachian Consciousness

October 3

Our first encounter with the children was a catastrophe. It all started with the world "Bullshit." The students were herded into the industrial arts classroom by the principal after lunch. Many of the thirty-four children approached the room with a sense of fear and apprehension of the unknown. Some of them asked, as they approached the room, whether or not they were going to be paddled because they were bad.

We had placed thirty-four chairs in a circle and only one was occupied. They were lying upon saws and work tables, punching each other, yelling at each other, and refusing to look at any of us. It was an eerie feeling. They were in a state of confusion, but still I felt their lonely silence and their alienation from us. I was so scared; I felt if I made them sit down, they would get up and leave.

I attempted to explain to them the purpose of the program and how we were going to explore other ways of learning instead of the traditional learning environment. I was using words such as "humanitarian," "relationship," "conducive," etc., which didn't make any sense to them. My New York accent and the use of the vernacular "youse guys" were completely foreign to them. I just felt that I was not wanted and because of their limited vocabulary they were having trouble understanding involved sentences and nuances of wordings. They were sullen and uncommunicative but talkative within their peer groups. They refused to talk to me; only through their comments to their peers were they indirectly talking to me.

I told them that they were not a special-education class and not to feel that they were chosen as the bad kids of the school, and that they would be treated fairly and humanely, and they did not have to worry about being paddled in this program. This was a lie and they knew it. They were told that morning by their teachers that because of their behavior they were going to be put into a special-education area. Once they diagnosed my lie, the rumbling and noise level got louder and louder until I could not hear myself talk. I turned to a girl who was quite conscious of my lies and said I wanted to be her friend. She looked at me, and without a sign of emotion, said, "Bullshit."

This was the signal that set the industrial arts room into a climate of uncontrollable chaos. I just realized that these youngsters do not learn to listen to what words mean but only to what emotion the speaker conveys. They hear the feeling behind the words. What they were really hearing, was my saying to them, we know you're a special discipline class, but you are too dumb to realize it, so we won't admit this fact to you.

I didn't have time to admit this lie because I was too scared that someone was going to get hurt with the tools in the industrial arts room which were now being used as swords and missiles. Once I collected my emotional forces, the rest of the teachers and I broke the large group into small groups of five to seven and went to different parts of the school in an attempt to get to know the students and for them to get to know us better. We wanted to find what interested them and how we could supply the resources to satisfy their interests. They refused to tell us about their feelings and could care less how we felt. What we did find out was that they liked hiking, exploring old caves and abandoned cars and houses, hunting, fishing, and raising hell. They wanted activities that provided physical and emotional outlets. In addition, because the group of kids were from seventh to ninth grade, they were also interested in finding out about sex, marriage, and birth control. I also felt that the boys had to be masculine and the girls were supposed to submit to the desires of the boys. They could care less about abstract ideas or principles such as mathematics and the study of government.

On the way out of the school, I encountered Pete, one of our students. He was considered the strong guy of the school and did not take any shit from any of the teachers. He was the titular leader of the students who came from working-class homes. I noticed during our afternoon session that he was sullen and stoic and refused to respond to our requests to participate in activities. He had deep set eyes which were crossed and I never knew when he had his eyes focused. He was respected by the guys because of his strength and by the girls because he was masculine.

He started to speak to me as I approached him. "Hey Mister Doctorate. School, ain't no way going to work for us in that program. We're too stupid and dumb. My daddy says the only people stupider than us is the niggers. All the teachers in this school say we're too stupid to learn so they get rid of us by putting us in your program for dummies. They don't want no stupid kids around. They even say we dress and smell different than the pretty kids of the school whose parents are all rich. These kids are the teachers' pets. This school is a pain in the ass and I hate it. I bet if you stay around you'll beat us just like the other teachers. Don't waste your time with us folks, we don't want you. We got enough problems—we don't need any long-haired hippie do-gooder."

After this last sentence he turned and left with his friends, while walking away he gave me the peace sign and then the finger.

>
> Thoughts move like things distant
> in memory through the shadow
> gardens of my past wandering.
>
> Tongues move inside me
> yet I cannot speak.
>
> The images before my eyes
> are of no concern,
> for they are mockery
> of visions I have seen.

> Is there worse starvation
> than hunger for expression
> finding no medium?
>
> I am a lake of water filling
> with no outflowing.
>
> Is there greater emptiness
> than the mind of your listener
> whose thoughts go another way
> leaving you to find your way
> alone?
>
> Walter Willard Price

October 4

This morning we attempted to translate some of the data we collected from them during the memorable first day. We decided that we would establish different project areas: one would be writing plays; one would be exploring the outside lands and hills. Basically, we wanted the students to work in things they were interested in; let them exhaust this interest, and then find other interests when they were ready. We felt we could build the basic skills like reading, writing, mathematics, and science around these interests. I felt so proud of our planning and I just knew John Holt, George Dennison, and other critics of our school system would be proud of us. Yet, I had an uneasy feeling, for I felt we were being seduced by our interests and not the students'. Except for the area dealing with the outside I felt they were getting the same thing they get in schools, except we dressed it up a little bit more.

When the kids came this afternoon we had them go to their areas of interest. After about twenty minutes, all hell broke loose, and we had three hours to go before they were to leave for home. On top of this, the principal and teachers from the regular school came into our areas and complained about the noise and control of our students. Their complaints were not important to me at that moment, but what to do with these kids for three hours when our projects failed? We asked them what they wanted to do and they wanted to go outside to play games and explore the hills. They went out with us and we played right along with them and at times taught new games when they requested them. I recognized we were far from being accepted; however, what I did notice was the importance of their reference group, peers with whom the individual felt comfortable and accepted. They wanted to be accepted as a member of a reference group. They want to be liked, identified with, and noticed in their reference groups. Outside of their reference groups, they were suspicious of us.

That their lives in the hills were important to them was quite evident in the group that went to the woods to explore the environment with Jack. They came back and decided they were going to build a terrarium and study the relationships of animal and man to his environment. I could just sense the excitement and happiness they felt inside themselves.

In addition, as we played along with them, talking to them and not down to them as the first day, they started to talk about themselves. Communication between us and students was not extensive but it was long enough to put some handles on how they thought and felt. Thus, some of their stoic behavior was starting to break down. I was particularly struck by the extremely limited training they had had in verbal skills.

I remember meeting two beautiful young girls who were twins and could only communicate with grins and groans. Sometime later, a social worker who was the only person allowed in the girls' home, found out that the parents were passive, dull, lifeless, and spoke in one-syllable words. Often when attempting to speak they spoke in baby talk. This seems impossible today with our media explosion, but to some degree this lack of nonverbal communication is true in the majority of Appalachian homes. It may explain our lack of success in getting the kids in our program to participate in large group discussion. They just have not had the experience in verbalizing. Their schooling up to this point has reinforced their lack of nonverbal behavior; in the schools they have attended, as is true throughout the country, the teacher does most of the talking in the classroom.

At the end of the day, two teachers from the regular school approached me and complained that their students could see us outside their windows, which in turn made them very restless. One teacher said, "A child is not supposed to enjoy and have fun while learning—it's hard work like the coal mines." The other teacher suggested that if we went outside again it would be best for the rest of the school if we stayed out of sight of her kids because it would be too tempting for them. (*School—ain't no way . . .*)

Today we were also able to collect some data on how they felt about themselves as persons by drawings we asked them to do regarding how they felt others perceived them. The drawings seemed to indicate that the child of Appalachia lacks a sense of who he is and where he is going. The common response to what are you going to do when you leave school was either work in the mines, join the army, or get married. They have had very little experience with other occupations such as: engineering, aviation, computer technicians, management, etc. Basically the lower class Appalachian is primarily concerned with the present, not with the future. This is true of any working-class culture and its children. Similar characteristics could be found in the north end of Boston, and within many other ethnic groups in urban areas. Thus, many of these children didn't mention materialistic goals when asked, but usually rejected these goals. They were concerned only with having "enough" to get by.

Jack Weller oversimplified the problems of Appalachia and the character of its people. He implies that they are fatalistic, nonambitious, deprived, and not able to fit into middle-class culture. I only found them fatalistic or nonambitious when someone was forcing values, life styles, and schedules on them, a normal enough reaction for people made to do something contrary to their wills. It seems Jack Weller and others like him who have written about the area, use, unvaryingly, a middle-class standard to evaluate the people of Appalachia and I think this is where the problem lies. It is not so much within the people but within those who evaluate using an inapplicable or misused set of criteria. This group of evaluators includes sociologists, educators, politicians, various researchers, and federal agencies—the high priests of mainstream middle-class culture—who, through their research perpetuate a monolithic concept of society.

How do we develop a learning environment to work within a working class of Appalachian culture and its characteristics? I thought I had the answer before I started; now I feel naked. It may be as their culture unfolds I'll be better able to do this—God, I hope so. How do we develop a learning environment which doesn't destroy their uniqueness and culture and doesn't force them to reject their culture and accept WASP values?

October 5

Realizing the importance of their reference groups, their low self-concepts, their uniqueness, and their interests in outdoor activities, I decided we must somehow tie these interests into what we were doing in the program. I was thinking about these problems this morning during my drive to the school. I became enthralled with the aesthetics and the beauty of the West Virginia hills, especially the color, which is indescribable, during the fall season. Its beauty was breathtaking and so overcoming that I could forget the trash, garbage, and litter on the highways. This drive reminds me of the roads in Vermont which twist and turn and at each turn is a new adventure with nature. I wonder if the Appalachian child did not have to go to school what he would do? Probably, he would go hiking, hunting, and fishing.

I really envy them—what the hell could I offer them in school? In many respects they already had what I and others like me are searching for in order to get away from our technological society. When I thought about what I could offer these children, I reached the conclusion—very little. The prospective teachers and I have been spending most of our time in institutions getting degrees with very little opportunity for encountering life and having experiences with today's world. As I was reaching this conclusion, I noticed that I was approaching the school. Its architecture was rectangular and it was composed of one large hallway with classrooms on both sides, a cafeteria, and a beautiful gym. It was quite evident by the magnitude of the gym and the amount of time given to not only sports but to bands how important these activities were to the community. In many school systems throughout West Virginia there is not enough money to buy materials for schools, but there is always money available for basketball floors, football fields, and band uniforms and instruments. These activities provide an escape from the Appalachian life and both parents and children can forget their troubles in the emotional and vicarious experience of a good basketball or football game. (If Jerry West would run for governor of this state he would be elected by an overwhelming majority of people.) That's another story.

Behind the school were four portable classrooms which were used for the elementary school. If the children needed to go to the bathroom or get a drink or go to lunch, they had to go outside before entering the main building. I've heard that some of the elementary teachers during the winter months would make a child stand outside as his punishment. Paradoxically, the school is surrounded by forty beautiful acres of almost unspoiled West Virginia hills and forest; however, the outside rarely ever becomes a major part of the regular school curriculum.

To get to the Boiler Room, I had to pass through the gym. On the way to the Boiler Room, I became aware of the fact that when the kids got off the bus they had to go straight to gym and stay there until the bell rang to go to their homerooms. This meant that at times some kids were locked in there for forty minutes. They were allowed to play games; however, have you ever tried to play basketball or volleyball with two hundred kids running all over the gym floor? The kids were locked up in the gym and the teachers stood guard at the entrance to make sure no one got out. All I could think of was that these kids were like tigers locked up and waiting to be set free to enter their separate cages or cells when the signal was given. Is this a school or a concentration camp? The kids were being treated as prisoners or animals, hence they were acting like animals. They were screaming, yelling, fighting, cursing. My God, was it crazy. As I walked through, kids were hanging on me and seemed to be saying get us the hell out of here. I just wanted to scream. But I didn't for obvious reasons. If I screamed, "Fuck it," I would be out! And then the system wins and the kids and myself lose to the one dimensionality of schools, again.

In the Boiler Room I noticed the toilet was leaking urine through the wall that separates the Boiler Room from the thoroughfare. Besides the leak, there must have been five million flies around the room, because it was cold outside and the Boiler Room was the warmest place to be. The principal stopped in to remind us about the policy of the school concerning the kids chewing gum. He felt this type of behavior must be kept in check. (*School—ain't no way . . .*)

Our school activities that we planned for today worked for about twenty minutes, until some of the prospective teachers felt that the students needed remedial work in reading, writing, mathematics—they started to play teacher—all shit broke loose again. So, as we did the previous day, we went outside with them and became their friends again and not teachers.

How do you play both roles? Can it be done? Is school an anathema to the Appalachian child's culture?

October 9

Today I brought to the planning session some new games such as Monopoly, matho, Cuisenaire rods, basketball and football games, puzzles, Play Doh, segments of elementary science projects, number-painting sets, checkers, and different magazines such as *Sports Illustrated, Field and Stream, U. S. News and World Report*, and *Time.* We realized the majority of the kids were deficient in the basic skills of reading, writing, and mathematics. We also realized that they worked better with concrete ideas than with abstract ideas. Thus, we felt if we could get them involved in games and projects that were interesting to them, they might be motivated enough to acquire some of these basic skills.

During our morning planning session some of the kids in our project asked me to come with them in order to stop Mr. Prate from paddling some fifteen boys. "He's gone crazy!" When I encountered Mr. Prate, he was on his way out of the gym and he related to me that he paddled these people because they didn't want to participate in gym activities. His speech was couched in very nervous nuances and it seemed to me he wanted to rid himself of some guilt. His basic thesis revolved around the idea that we need "to humiliate children in order that they may become better human beings." (*School—ain't no way . . .*)

During our school's activities, some kids were playing

the different games; others were working on the terrarium. Others were working on a play about which I knew very little; Bill was handling this project area. Jane was with those who were interested in working with paints and other art projects.

Some of the kids who were working with games were the ones who could not add, subtract, divide, or write more than a sentence, etc. They were learning while also having fun.

Things were really going great until the band started to play in the gym. The painter who was attempting to paint the doors of the Boiler Room was coming in and out of the Boiler Room to mix his paints; in addition, the janitor was burning trash in the incinerator. The principal also came in because he couldn't find a student and he thought maybe I had seen him. It turned into a funny farm. Thus, the kids wanted to listen to the band and we thought it was a good idea, especially since the Boiler Room had become Grand Central Station. However, what I forgot was that the band members were the well behaved of the school and were from either middle-class or upper-middle-class homes of the community. They were usually condescending to the kids in our project and hence our kids thought they were snobbish and "uppity." After about twenty minutes of listening to the band, our kids started to run in and out of the band which I thought was quite funny. But we had to stop them because fights started to break out and we were scared someone would get hurt.

We went out to the hills, again. I've noticed that the Appalachian child will only work when "he is in the mood for it." Specifically, I've observed when we forced the kids into a tight schedule they usually rebelled by becoming quite stoic and sullen, and refused to do anything. This is also true of his parents who usually paced his life according to different seasons or times of the year instead of the business day or week. He is quite moved during the hunting and fishing seasons or the gardening seasons. In the spring his children are quite moved to play in the hills and explore old caves and mines.

I think one of the reasons that companies in Detroit which have assembly-line production consider Appalachians bad workers is because the hill person takes many breaks, takes off a day or two a week, talks with his co-workers, etc. All of these behaviors are contrary to making a good assembly-line worker.

This afternoon I sat down with Dave, Pete, and Gary, who were still floundering in the program and considered by the rest of the school as hopeless cases. I didn't mind their floundering or their hiding in the crawl way under the school for a smoke when they were supposed to be with us. I realize now the importance for them to be accepted in their reference groups and I was wishing I knew how to use reference group orientation while tapping some of their interests. We sat ourselves down in the grass and I was determined to be completely honest with them and to talk about anything they wanted to talk about. They were also honest with me and I just felt like they enjoyed talking to me about their home lives, sex, drinking, drugs, girls, hunting, and their cars. We spent the rest of the afternoon talking about their feelings, perceptions and attitudes concerning these areas. I learned a hell of a lot from them. They told me about their little brothers and sisters and about how important they are in the families. However, they felt when they started to go to school their parents as Pete said, "Don't give a shit." If they do something wrong they "get the hell beaten out of them" by either their fathers or mothers. Even though there is a feeling of hate for parents, they still admitted they loved their parents very much. The family is a closely knit unit in Appalachia, for they told me about older brothers and sisters and grandparents all living in the same house. They are constantly preached at about behaving like an adult. That is, their culture seems to be adult centered and children must learn very quickly how to behave as adults. They mentioned many nights go by when very few words pass between themselves and their family or between their mother and father. Pete said the only time his parents talk to him is when his father wants him to change the TV station or wants another beer. It seems that because of this type of climate very few social skills are learned. They mentioned they never talked about controversial issues at home or with their friends because of the fear of creating a conflict which might put their position in the reference group or in the family in jeopardy.

Gary said something that was quite interesting. He said, "I don't care how hard somebody paddles me if I deserve it. I don't like it to be made fun of, then I get mad."

Pete also explained to me why he hated niggers. It was a long involved story starting with a drinking escapade and driving around with one of his buddies looking for a fight. To make a long story short, he went on to tell me how he got into a fight with a nigger and he said, "I whipped his ass—" He felt because the black person fought dirty that "niggers were like animals," which also supported his father's feeling concerning black people. What is most interesting about this conversation is not Pete's prejudice and ultraconservatism, but when he or his friends during the conversation were making a point or arguing, they never used abstractions but used storytelling or anecdotes.

As we were walking out to go to a general meeting of the children and teachers of the Boiler Room School, I put my arm over John and he twitched, thinking first I was going to hit him, but I think he realized it was a friendship hug and I could feel that he was astonished that maybe I could be his friend.

A so-called community meeting of the Boiler Room School was called for the last hour of the school day so we could discuss the students' and teachers' problems and attempt to reach some sort of decision. We had decided that if something came up for a vote, everyone, both teachers and students, would have equal votes.

We never got past talking how we would chair the meetings. No one would give opinions or assume a leadership role. The kids refused to take a stand on any issue. They were talking or punching their friends and they refused to make any decisions or give any direction we might move into. If someone attempted to take a leadership role the rest of his reference group made fun of him until he abated this role. It was noisy, however, in a way, it was the silence of their opinions and their refusing to take leadership roles which really bothered me.

As we were talking about sharing and caring, Ted Williams, a seventh grader who was in our program and who had difficulty with speaking and reading and was classified by many teachers as the "Special Ed. kid," came into the room crying. I thought this would be a beautiful opportunity for the others to show love and concern for a fellow human being. Their responses were cruel and critical as I found out in my previous discussions with Pete and others. "He deserves whatever happened to him." "He's stupid." "The teachers call him stupid." In the midst of this verbal slaughter of Ted Williams, his crying got louder and louder. Then Ted said, "You all shit on me all the time." (*School—ain't no way . . .*)

October 10

I felt we were starting to get to know the kids better and their culture as well. Our major purpose during planning sessions was no longer to play teacher but to learn how to design and collect materials which would help develop their interests. We decided from today on that we were going to try to stop playing teacher—even though we realized that we had to decondition ourselves because of our miseducation. It was also decided that we would really try to learn about their culture and not to attempt to force our middle-class values upon them. We must learn to cope with their values and also begin to have some tolerance for turbulence. I felt what we were really trying to do was to learn how to release the potential and culture that existed in each one of the kids in our program.

During our Boiler Room School activities the climate was warm, exciting, and interesting to watch. Mostly, it was the teacher who was having the difficulty today. Some of the kids had finished building the terrarium and were now painting it, while others were collecting materials and small animals to live in it. Others were getting ready to video tape their play. Others were working on different art projects such as stonecraft, burlap stitchery, foil craft, paper mosaics, and drawing pictures, while others were still floundering, searching, and seeking ideas. These people we kept bombarding with different ideas, hoping that maybe we would hit upon one that they would want to get into.

Pete, Gary, John, and Greg still could not get into anything. They liked talking about their lives: However, once they encountered anything that resembled English or mathematics, they got completely turned off. I did find out today that they liked to hang around gas stations and work on cars. Gary mentioned that his dad was a used-car dealer and he had a '65 Chevy he wanted to get rid of and he and the rest of the guys thought it would be a great idea to have it at the school in order to work and learn about cars for their project activities. I had a couple of the project's teachers go with Gary and pick up the car from his father. Afterward, Jerry told me what happened when they approached the father and asked for the car. The father looked at his son and at the car and said to Jerry, "Get the fucking car out of here."

The car was placed in the back of the school next to the garbage cans. The guys were really thrilled and you just felt good for them. We had found an interest for those guys and they decided they would be called the Motor Pool Gang. They just couldn't believe that they were going to rebuild a motor without nobody taking it away from them. I told them I would remember to get car manuals, books on the internal combustion engine, but they decided they would bring these in. I'm glad because as I told them, I know nothing about cars and would learn right along with them. Another thing that stands out in my mind this day was the feeling that one of the teachers, Bill, was saying a lot of things which were couched in pomposity or "bullshit." He seemed to always have great ideas but refused to develop them. In addition, I felt the other teachers were getting upset because he wasn't accepting the responsibility for developing and implementing materials for the Boiler Room School. He seemed to be a braggart and was talking about how he was able to cope with the extreme hardships of the Peace Corps and VISTA. (I am starting to doubt the veracity of these stories.) But, the kids seemed to like him because he was entertaining and different. Yet, he seemed to be like many of the students at the university level who claim to be on the radical left and make up slogans using Marcuse's and Marx's ideas, yet when they are confronted to develop these ideas more "in depth" they become defensive. On the other hand, maybe this feeling I have about Bill is not true.

Besides this, I noticed that Jane seems to be more scared of the kids than anyone else and she doesn't seem to want to reach out. Maybe because she is so prim and proper and comes from a different background, her WASP values are coming into conflict with the kids. Our kids are smelly at times, wear the same clothes sometimes a whole year, and are very physical and emotional which really turns Jane off. Her missionary zeal is waning. The other three student teachers are still having the same difficulty with the idea of not playing teacher but being a friend, a guide to the student. They are still groping with my definition of freedom. I told them that I felt a student needs many creative alternative choices available to him in a learning situation. Once he is able to select by his own volition an alternative, he then exercises his freedom. They felt the students in exercising their choices were too noisy and at times were confused. I told them before any lasting change takes place we must have a period of "controlled chaos" and we must build up a tolerance for the "controlled chaos" period. They were trying, but when this tolerance weakened, they reverted to the yelling and to the threatening of students which they knew didn't work. But it made them comfortable to have something to fall back on.

The saddest of all this is what I noticed today: how some of the teachers in the school building treated the project teachers. They were treated as outcasts and were being constantly hassled by the principal because they didn't know how to control the classroom. The principal still could not understand what we were trying to do and he couldn't understand why our kids were not sitting in rows and only talking when they were given permission. Why can't he understand that we're creating another type of learning environment? It's this type of administrator and teachers like him who cause kids to say as Pete tells me almost everyday, "This school sucks."

October 13

We have noticed that the children we are working with have no self-confidence when it comes to writing and doing simple math problems. Thus, we decided we would give them many opportunities to just write without the fear of making grammatical mistakes. Similarly, we did the same thing with the other project areas. These children as we found out earlier need a great deal of emotional support and encouragement because, as their fathers and mothers act, they won't do something unless they're quite confident that it will be a success. Once they realized that we were not going to criticize them for their work, they got involved in all sorts of things. We only gave them help when they asked for it. As they were feeling comfortable and not embarrassed to ask questions of us, they started to ask all sorts of questions. They ranged from how do you spell West Virginia, their brothers' and sisters' names, the month they were born in, to their friends' names. They also asked basic questions in math such as how many pennies in a dollar, how to subtract or divide using a remainder. I imagine these questions have been bothering some of these children for years, but because of the fear of being considered stupid by the teachers and peers, they just sat there for seven to nine years not saying anything.

There was the same kind of success building with the Motor Pool Gang. They had stripped the motor down and were attempting to understand the inner workings of the internal combustion engine. They looked at pictures in a book and picked up the parts which the book was explaining. They had difficulty reading in front of their peers because they had never grasped some of the basic skills in phonics. What I did was praise them when they were able to finish a sentence or a word they didn't know. After a while I could see that they knew I wasn't going to make fun of them and their friends weren't going to make fun of them, because they were too interested in finding out about engines. Thus, as was happening in the other areas, they had been motivated by their interest to learn something on their own, and when they were stuck they reached out for our help.

Besides this success building with the project kids, I also sat down with Pete who was not feeling good about himself today. He was perplexed by the fact that many teachers in the regular school and people outside the community considered him a hillbilly because of his speech. As mentioned previously, many of these children lack a sense of self and can only identify themselves in relationship to their reference group. He kept repeating to me in our conversation, "I'm just an old hillbilly," and on and on he degraded himself. What I did may sound cruel to somebody but I wrote on a piece of paper some of the words he used like "feller," "holler," "goin," "comin," "seein," "fur," "cur," and then in another column I wrote the correct pronunciation, fellow, hollow, going, coming, seeing, far, car. After that I wrote the phonological variation of his dialect. I found some old Sunday newspapers which usually had a supplement with poems written by local townspeople. In many of these poems, the Appalachian dialect is used. He examined these poems very carefully and also a book that had been lying around the school consisting of mountaineer poems. After about ten minutes he said, "You mean they write like I talk." I said, "It's okay how someone speaks as long as we understand each other." Pete wanted to take the book of poems home to his parents to show them that even people like himself write beautiful poems.

Meanwhile, I was thinking, why the hell do the teachers of Appalachia completely overlook the culture of their students. There are voluminous amounts of folk songs, poems, and stories left by their ancestors, and most of them collect dust in a library or on the shelves of McClain Printing Company. Ken McClain in the last fifteen years has done more to conserve the culture of Appalachia in West Virginia than anyone else; however, few recognize this. They have a beautiful Appalachian culture which should give them a sense of identity and pride but the typical Appalachian teacher refuses to recognize the potential of this culture. They seem ashamed of it. The typical Appalachian teacher and school usually epitomizes the middle-class or WASP values, and forces these values on the children of Appalachia until the child is forced to reject his culture and accept WASP values. Under the facade of "progress" schools destroy their culture.

Lastly, I noticed today that Bill and his play group were coming apart at the seams. It seems they were attempting to put on a play about the ape man on the moon and they just couldn't relate to it at all. Maybe, it would have been better if they had developed their own play and not anyone else's. I must talk to Bill about this idea tomorrow.

October 23

Lately, the Boiler Room has become our planning and meeting room, laboratory and resource room, a crying room, a shelter for different animals, a dressing room for the Motor Pool Gang, a storage room, etc. In short, the Boiler Room is our home base and we are most comfortable in it.

In our planning session today we decided to open the classroom climate up and have many more choices available for the students to make. We were hoping that this would give the students an opportunity to work with freedom and accept more of the responsibility for their own.

We saturated the three rooms we were using by increasing the number of learning centers in each of these rooms. What I was hoping to do was to use the English developed concept of the informal curriculum. That is, find the child's interest and integrate with this interest skills in mathematics, English, science, social studies, etc. We were hoping after their interest was exhausted we would guide them to another interest or learning center. If a child wanted to build his own learning center we thought this was great. Each center had a poster with directions for the student in order to help him get involved with the center: in addition, there were materials that were related to the purpose of the center. There was also a task for each student to accomplish before he moved on to other learning centers. We also selected materials that we felt different individual students could work with. We gave the Cuisenaire rods set to Lou Taylor because of the difficulty he was having learning how to add and subtract and we gave Ted Williams some burlap, yarn, and needle so that through tactile experience he might learn how to make letters and also write his name. They were allowed to stay with these interests as long as they wanted to. I found out after school that one of the teachers, Jack, got the "hell scared out of him" by a garden snake on his collecting tour in the woods with his learning center group.

The learning center idea in conjunction with the ongoing long term projects seemed to be going fairly well for about an hour. Then it got to be chaotic and what we started to experience was sloppy permissiveness. What happened today was similar to people attending a state or county fair. They spent the whole day looking at the exhibits and demonstrations without ever getting involved. A basic problem was not the kids, but the teachers, again, who during this hour, spent the majority of their time standing up in a corner of the room just looking and not interacting with the kids. They felt that the kids would get involved on their own without any help from them. A child cannot turn himself on and off to different environments. Although for the last four weeks we had been giving them more choices on their own, they could not in one day take over completely on their own. It is very difficult to lose the conditioning of seven to nine years of what is usually an autocratic classroom climate and suddenly adjust to an open classroom climate. It's almost impossible.

Another incident which happened today was a fight between Kathy and Mike. This took place after about ten minutes in our learning center activity. Before we were able to break up the fight Kathy gave Mike a black eye and he kicked her so hard that it split open her leg. After I was able to pull them apart, we took a walk together so they could settle down. I started to look for an available space so that we could talk privately and I found the principal's office not being used. In sort of a Ham Ginott fashion I let them vent their feelings and fed it back to them. This usually saves a great deal of time for if someone doesn't identify the feelings behind hostile behavior, then the discussion of the incident turns into an exercise of superficialities. All feelings behind the incident must be brought to the surface. In this case, the major feelings identified were anger and hostility against each other. Kathy didn't like Mike because he was always picking on small kids and vice versa; Mike didn't like Kathy because she was quite masculine. I imagined she must have weighed something like 160 pounds and it wasn't fat, it was muscle.

Both Kathy and Mike started to get into a discussion about "loving thy enemy." They both got emotional and started to cry. Before I knew it they were apologizing to each other and both felt with God's help they could learn to live with each other. The most interesting aspect of this incident was that once these children realized they had hurt someone's feelings, they felt bad and then they wanted to make amends. Many times when they're being critical or fighting they don't realize that sometimes they are hurting people.

It seems that even though we were having some difficulty with the learning center and in spite of my encounter with Mike and Kathy, one of the teachers, Jack, felt good about today. The following are some quotes taken from his diary for today:

"It was really great today to watch the kids learn to use a ruler in measuring for their terrarium. I realized they didn't know how to use it, but their need made them want to learn.

"Another bright spot was watching Betty and John work together and show a real interest in doing math problems. I watched two human beings help each other. More people should realize the power of this."

October 28

There was no school today; however, we were requested to attend a regular school staff meeting that morning to discuss the progress of the project. I think the real reason was some of the members of the regular school faculty wanted to relieve their hostility and criticism about the program. Moreover, they wanted to discuss with us the method we were going to use in evaluating the project students.

During the meeting, several things were brought to my attention. Some of the teachers felt that the kids in the program didn't know who was boss and that some of the kids who were doing well in the project had been awful in their classes. They felt some of the kids were skipping classes and hiding in the morning, only coming to our program in the afternoon. One of the teachers who was involved in the program for one day said after spending a day with us, he got so upset at the lack of control and noise in our program he had to go home to take tranquilizers. Then he really blew his cool, "Schools are for teachers." "Your program is not structured enough." "I refuse to be abused by students." "My room was dirty and had papers on the floor when I came back to it after your teacher was in here for a day." "Your teachers don't know how to keep rooms clean." He had more things to say but I guess the above statements are the gist of it. Finally, he got up, with a coffee cup in his hand—I was sure he was going to throw it at me. He didn't; he just got up shaking and left the room.

I felt depressed, not from his remarks but because I knew day after day he was encountering youngsters and what type of damage he has done and what he is presently doing. Yet, the public school system could not get rid of him, for he was a strong supporter of their goals.

After the outbreak, I think the rest of the faculty was sort of embarrassed and they felt sorry for me. What they didn't know was that if I hadn't realized the project was at stake, I would have probably shot the guy and saved thousands of kids from being destroyed by him. After second thoughts, I don't think I would have shot him because there are many more like him and it is not going to make that much difference. Wow! That's logical thinking isn't it?

The faculty, after some debate, gave us permission to not assign grades, since junior high grades don't really count, but we were allowed to give an individual report on each student according to our perceptions of his growth. We also decided that we would back up this individual report with a file consisting of our observations and the materials which the student had produced. Ours and the student's observations of his progress would be the heart of the evaluation. I thought this method was one of the better ways of coping with the "grading syndrome."

One thing this meeting did accomplish was to pull the Boiler Room teachers closer together, except for Bill who did not show up. I believe we need this closeness in order to survive in the public school system which has a built-in mechanism to suppress any alternative which deviates from its norms. One needs to have allies on the regular school staff. We had two, Betty and Jim. Betty and Jim would come in once or twice a week to work in our project while the project student teachers would take their places in the regular classroom. Betty was a warm, sensitive, honest person who intuitively understood these children and had a prodigious amount of empathy for them. She felt we were her support because she was waging a losing battle with many of the other teachers and the principal to do something about the regular school curriculum. I also noticed many of the ideas we were using in the project were filtrating back to her classroom. On the other hand, Jim was a former athlete, who, because of a bad injury, never had a chance to make it big. The kids understood this and because he was the coach of the basketball team he was able to relate to them without any problems at all. Another thing that is very important, a coach in Appalachia, especially in West Virginia, is treated as a god. In many communities the coaches make more money than the mathematics or history teacher. There might be no money for laboratory equipment or library books but, if the coach in an Appalachian community wants a new set of uniforms for his ballplayers, he'll get them some way or another from the community. Anyway, Jim was quite suspicious of us at the beginning and rejected the program. After about four weeks he decided that we were for real and not just the snobbish or uppity people from the big university. A feeling of trust was only built up by Jim's stopping in for coffee and planning sessions, going out to lunch with us, etc. Once he accepted us as part of his reference group and saw us as friends, he started to trust us and get involved with us in the same way as Betty did once or twice a week. The other teachers in the school building refused to get involved in our project. Nevertheless, Betty's and Jim's support was what was needed in order to combat the opposing forces in the rest of the school.

November 3

I blew my cool in our morning planning session. In many respects, it became a catharsis for both me and the teachers. We laid everything out on top of the table that was bothering us. They felt that lately they had become dependent on me to supply them with ideas and materials. They agreed that it was much easier to shed responsibility for designing curriculum because the responsibility brings with it many conflicts and frustrations. Similarly, I realized that for four years they had been sitting on their asses in education courses and that in six or seven weeks it was quite an arduous task to do an about-face and start being active and taking on the responsibility for helping thirty-four children. In short they have been prepared to perpetuate the teacher image they have seen for over sixteen years. It was difficult for them to stop playing the "teaching and schooling game."

As I look back on this session, I think it was exactly what we needed to get moving again. The pressures of the school's constraints and constant turbulence created by children learning to cope with their new found freedom is physically and psychologically exhausting at times.

Possibly, this session had something to do with the learning that took place later on in our project today. It was fantastic! They really seemed to be having fun today, also learning. Some kids were writing their own stories; others were working on the car; others were working on the terrarium; others were building a volcano; others were just playing games like checkers and Monopoly; others were just daydreaming. I believe for the first time they felt they had some control over their environment and they were learning how to make choices for themselves.

In addition, I observed that some of the kids who took a walk in the woods with me were adventure oriented. They loved to take chances, like seeing whether or not they could make it across a stream by stepping on some small rocks without falling in. They told me how they would explore old mines and caves and it was fun because there was always a constant danger of these things caving in. They related stories how in a nearby lake they would fight the rapids in old boats. Concomitantly, I also observed that many of the kids, especially the Motor Pool Gang, loved to get physically involved with things. The more physical, the better off they felt. It seems to me, because of this adventure oriented attitude, that the whole schooling in Appalachia has very little of interest for their culture. (*School—ain't no way . . .*) This is a result of the academic or college orientation of many of the schools in the Appalachian region. There is an enormous need to recognize this fact.

It's quite evident to me that the same adventure orientation of the Appalachian student can be traced to his father's occupation. The majority of our kids' fathers were in occupations such as coal mining, construction, truck driving, drilling, strip-mining, etc. These types of occupations lend themselves to adventures or action-oriented behavior. This is especially true of coal mining.

An adventure or physical orientation also was apparent in our creative movement exercise. Precisely, we were trying to break out of the traditional physical education curriculum of playing basketball, soccer, football, etc. To do this we had the kids get into circles of about four or five and then put on records of their own fast country or rock music. After this we asked them to pretend they had things like a medicine ball, a broken egg, an ice cube, yo-yo, basketball, or were walking on the moon. Then we asked them to do anything they wanted to do with this object. It was really beautiful and comical to watch these kids use their minds and bodies creatively. I had Jim run these activities and he was quite skeptical at first and then after seeing the results he was quite enthusiastic about the whole thing. A latent effect of this activity was that boys and girls were not separated as in traditional physical education classes, and many of the sex stereotypes that exist in Appalachia began to be broken down. The teachers were also involved in these exercises which also helped to break down more barriers between teachers and students.

One final note, Bill was not here today and it seems lately every other day he's taking two days off. I feel the group knows something about him but is reluctant to reveal it to me. Perhaps, the reality of the situation in the Boiler Room and his rhetoric are in conflict. It may be withdrawal behavior. The situation may be too difficult for him and the way he is adapting to it, is by withdrawing physically and psychologically. I just don't know.

November 5

I started today to have group counseling sessions composed of four or five students to explore their difficulties and to give mutual emotional support to one another. This was moving very nicely with the kids until the principal interrupted today's session and told me to look down the hall. I could see one teacher standing in front of his door with his hands on his hips just steaming mad. I walked to him and the first thing he said was, "Those dummies better clean up the grease they tramped in here right now." I calmly asked two of the fellows from the Motor Pool Gang to give me a hand in cleaning it up. Then, Gary and I got on our knees and started helping to clean it up. The look on this teacher's face, when I got down to help Gary, was a sight to behold. After we cleaned it up and left, he slammed the door. At the same time Gary called him a "son of a bitch" and then Gary proceeded to tell how this teacher physically or mentally destroyed any student who deviated from the rules and regulations he set down. Thus, some of the guys who hated him would constantly hassle him, as by walking in his room with grease on their shoes because they knew he had a thing about "cleanliness."

On the way back to the motor pool area, Gary turned to me and said in a sort of hushed voice, "At least you are willing to listen to us and treat us like real people, the rest of the son of a bitches in this school treat us like dogs." This was the first time in seven weeks that one of the hard-core types started to reach out to me—I was ecstatic.

My good feeling was coupled with some good results in the group counseling sessions where the kids were really trying to look at themselves. I felt pretty good at this point, that is until I encountered Bill later on in the afternoon.

The first thing he said when he met me was, "Well I might as well tell you what happened yesterday, you will probably hear about it from the others." He began to relate how he felt every one of the other teachers in the program was reaching a breaking point and they really wanted stronger means of punishment, such as paddling—I just couldn't believe it. Then he said, "I paddled Ted Williams yesterday because he deserved it. He punched another kid in the program." All I could say was, "My God—what the hell did you do to that child?" Then I went on to explain that Ted had come to us with difficulty in speaking and relating to other children and also was classified as a Special Education student. After about seven weeks in our project he was finally reaching out. He was just starting to get some tactile feeling for words and letters and was now able to write his name, which was impossible for him to do seven weeks ago. We also felt he was very physical, but he was starting to respect the rights of others and he didn't have to punch in order to get attention from us or his peers as before. Yet, Bill could not see that he destroyed him with the same type of behavior we were trying to eliminate. However, what hurt most of all was that he was always the one teacher in our group meeting who spoke about being human to children. He was not able to see beyond his bullshit or his fraudulence. He did admit that he was having some personal problems, also that he had a very violent temper and that he could not cope with frustrating or ambivalent situations. At the end of our conversation we decided for both the program's benefit and his that he should leave the program.

I think I've learned a valuable lesson from this experience with Bill—be suspicious of those who do a great deal of intellectualizing and who go around sloganeering. No longer in education can we afford to have around the Bills. They help to make the statement, *"School—ain't no way!"* true.

After my encounter with Bill I talked to the group of teachers after school about the "incident." I told them that I realized we were still adjusting to a new kind of role and learning environment. The children were also adjusting and at times fell back into old patterns when they become insecure in a new situation. I told them we must realize that going from an autocratic climate which existed in many of their homes and other classes to a more open, changing, and vulnerable one is not easy to accomplish overnight. However, helping children to develop respect through understanding and compassion is more permanent and lasting than paddling.

We decided that if we ever got in a situation where we wanted to hit the child we would leave until we gained our composure again. It was agreed that fight reaction, threats of punishment, or lost privileges don't accomplish anything. It was felt that if there were behavior problems that were disrupting the rights of others we either would bring the problem to the group's attention and have them solve it, or confront the problem and identify the feeling behind the behavior. If a youngster throws down his pencil and stomps out of the room we would not solve the real problem by yelling or threatening him to get back to the room, but we could say, "You feel frustrated don't you in doing those math problems." In the majority of instances the student will respond to this and will talk about his feeling of frustration.

At the end of our session, we decided that we also needed more preparation and more ideas so we decided to get together on a weekend. It seems that the incident with Bill and our talking about the discipline problems brought us even more closely together. I think our situation is similar to being in a family where we fight at times, love each other at times, have fun at times, but we are able to bring all elements into perspective in reaching for a common goal.

November 8

In the last seven weeks we have collected an enormous amount of materials and resources for our school. In addition, I have a bill of over two hundred dollars at one of the local stores where I purchased such things as games of Monopoly, Perquacky, Password, puzzles, Tumble Numble (math game), basketball and football games, paint sets (great for kids learning about numbers), Racko, dice, cards, Play Doh, model kits of the parts of the human body, and different model-car kits. We either used these things to develop learning centers or to help certain individuals in the program pick up some basic skills. For example, Password helps with word skills; Perquacky and Tumble Numble helps with math skills. Usually the situation defines for us how we are going to use the materials. Many of the children still get turned off with the learning environments as soon as we attach academic terminology.

One of the students brought in a black snake today and spent the whole day studying it and collecting reading materials from the library in order to gain an understanding of the snake's relationship to his environment. He felt the need, consequently, he initiated the study himself.

The Boiler Room is getting quite crowded with many different types of materials. Yet, we found out, the more materials or stimuli available, the more opportunities the children have to make choices on their own and to take responsibility for their learning. Speaking of their learning, I'm sure learning a hell of a lot about car engines and internal combustion since spending any free time working with the Motor Pool Gang. It was great to be co-learner in such a situation. The fellows like Greg, who, before the project began, was just waiting to turn sixteen to quit school now came regularly. However, since he has been in the project, his whole life both during and after school has been working on and thinking about the car. The reading, science, and mathematics integrated into their motor interest area have helped Greg and the others learn some basic skills. For example, Greg couldn't work with fractions until he needed to know how to measure the points setting in the ignition.

It was interesting to watch how they worked on the motor and how comfortable they were working around us. If they dropped something or did something wrong they would say something like "shit," "bitch," "piss," etc. The most important thing was that they were reacting and learning just the same as if they were working on some abandoned car near their homes.

Today, they asked me about the camshaft; of course I didn't know one damn thing about it. This surprised them, because they thought everyone with a doctorate should know everything there is to know about this world. (I was always being badgered by other kids in the regular school concerning their sicknesses, sprained ankles, etc.) As I said previously, I know very little of life after being schooled for something like twenty-two years.

After the fellows realized I didn't know anything about the camshaft, they asked Junie, the janitor who also worked in the Boiler Room. In the afternoon, he spent the majority of his time burning trash in the incinerator. (We were used to the smell and smoke that sometimes poured out of the incinerator.) He is a beautiful person, open, warm, compassionate, and he has an intuitive understanding of the mountaineer children. While he was explaining about the camshaft to the fellows, they were in a trance and gave him their utmost attention and respect. I watched him very carefully and he knew how to explain the complicated mechanism of the camshaft. I think sometimes the more schooling one has the stupider he gets. Maybe that's why teachers who get schooled are no longer able to communicate to youngsters. I think Junie is like many fathers in Appalachia. When they're showing their children how to hunt or fish, they don't get caught up in an exercise of pomposity. Perhaps the prospective teachers of Appalachia should go out and watch the parents of Appalachia and observe the teaching style they use with their children.

Meanwhile, as Junie was explaining to the fellows about the camshaft, I noticed that Pete and Gary were missing and at the same time I looked towards the woods and saw them running towards the woods as if something was wrong. I called to them and in unison they told me to go "fuck." Just then, the principal came in and told me that because Pete and Gary didn't have the right attitude in school that day they were paddled by him and another teacher. ("School—ain't going to work . . .") This paddling had destroyed within a period of five or ten minutes what we had created in Pete and Gary over a period of seven weeks. I must talk to Pete and Gary tomorrow to find out exactly what happened. Lastly, I'm really starting to feel guilty especially after the incident with Pete and

Gary because I can either go home or back to the womb of the university and escape the entrapment that exists in this school. But the kids in the Boiler Room cannot escape except by dropping out of school or getting lost in some hollow in Appalachia. Many times, they cannot escape by going home because their parents are caught in a larger entrapment of the corporate state. I think it is similar to those rich kids who call me from the suburbs of Boston or New York and relate to me how they want to help the poor people of Appalachia. Perhaps, one or two out of fifty are able to cope with the struggle in Appalachia. The dropouts escape by going home to their "super rich" communities or take off for a vacation to either Aspen, Bermuda, or Europe. Then, for the next four or five years, they'll talk about how they helped the poor people in Appalachia.

November 9

Gary was not in school today; he was suspended. However, Pete was in school and I was determined to talk to him concerning yesterday's incident. On my way to the Boiler Room I ran into Pete and Dave. Dave was a member of Pete's reference group and was quite lively and talkative in his own reference group. However, in the program he was shy, withdrawn, and lacked any sort of confidence to accomplish something.

I asked them to step into the Boiler Room where the terrarium stations were located. The students that were working with these stations were out in the woods collecting more materials and animals to put inside the terrarium.

As we sat down, Pete started to punch, hit, and fight

with Dave. I asked him what was wrong? He still kept fighting with Dave and pretended that he didn't hear a word I was saying. This went on for about twenty minutes until I asked Dave to sit across from Pete. This really pissed Pete off and I could see a power confrontation between Pete and me was coming.

He said, "Hey man, we don't want any long hair hippies to care for us—you're just doing it for a few weeks and then you'll leave us; so don't do us any favors by staying. We get the motor here and what happens? Everybody gets to work on it except me and Gary; so man get the fuck out of here. I don't want to be in any dummy class."

He started to get up and was ready to walk out when I asked if he would stay for a few more moments. He stalled and kicked something and said, "Mother fucker." At that point, I blew my cool. I went up to him staring into his eyes and said, "I really cared for you and loved you as a human being." Pete turned quickly and yelled on the way out to me, "Man you're a fucking queer."

November 10

Still not able to get over the shock of yesterday, I was met at the door by Pete, Gary, and Dave this morning. Pete said, "Hello, could I work with Jane today in art? I'd really like that." I responded bewilderedly, "Sure." It was like nothing had happened at all between us. They also wanted to go with me this morning to the university and find out about the place where I worked.

I received permission from the principal and started driving back towards the university with Pete, Dave, and Gary. During this trip, they really started to open up.

The tape deck was blasting with a hard rock group. It was Betty's car and she had all the latest hits on cassettes. Gary told me that he had never seen the university though he lived only a few miles away. In fact, Gary asked me what a campus was! They told me about their conception of university students and professors. In short, they felt university students were always rioting and their professors sat around stirring them up. Many of their ideas were from TV and their parents. In many respects, TV might be beneficial for the Appalachian person in finding out about the outside world. On the other hand, it may be detrimental to him because of his lack of education and intellectual sophistication. It is increasingly difficult for him to know what is true and what is propaganda in basic news reporting.

Pete mentioned that the university was no good because it didn't do anything for him. He was speaking about how the universities and government were no good if they didn't do something for him and his family. He said his dad said that, "The federal government is wasting lots of money on space trips and Vietnam and that this money should be shared by the 'people in West Virginia.' " I concurred!

We first stopped at the student center where many activities such as bowling, art shows, lectures, and protesting was held. While we were having coffee they were surprised to find out that the university students were not rioting. After we finished our coffee, we went outside and sat on one of the walls that surround the student center and watched the girls, people in general, and cars, in that order, as they passed us. They thought this was great and then they started to talk about whether or not they would like to attend such an institution. Gary and the others felt that they were too stupid to attend such an institution. We talked at great lengths about why they felt they were too stupid to go to a college. In addition, they didn't want the middle-class values, such as a nice house, car, clothes, and college education for their kids. They mostly wanted a job where they could make enough money to survive on and to go hunting and fishing and get drunk on the weekends with their friends.

The three refused to get on the elevator in the education building because they were afraid of it. It is ironical; they were so adventure oriented in the environment that is familiar to them, but they have a great fear of anything they don't know about that represents the outside world.

I brought them up to the office and just let them explore it awhile. They kidded me about my office and wanted to know if I sat on my ass all day. If you don't do anything physical or with your hands, they don't consider it work.

We left the education building and went over to a dormitory which was fairly new. I met Bob over there, who was a close friend and colleague and who filled in for me when I couldn't make it to the Boiler Room School because of my responsibilities at the university. He is an intelligent, articulate, and sensitive human being. He is not only concerned with the intellectual functions of education but is concerned with the other two, acting and feeling, which educators usually dismiss. Probably the most outstanding quality Bob possesses is his ability to relate to all kinds of people with different needs and abilities. Bob seems to have an innate ability for listening to an individual discuss his feelings and for making the individual feel that his feelings are also important to him. Bob took us to the basement of the dormitory and we got into a game of pool with Pete. Gary and Dave didn't want to play, but wanted to be on their own. Pete was quite a hustler; he beat me badly. Very evident was the gleam in his eyes because he just couldn't believe that here I was with a doctorate and I was a "shitty" pool player. This was great for him to see that I was human. This ecstatic feeling didn't last too long; he started to play Bob who had learned his pool well in the ghettos of Cincinnati. During the game, I could see that Bob was letting Pete beat him, but was still making it difficult for Pete to win. I think we both understood that Pete and the others needed as much success as they could get because of their low self-concept.

Meanwhile, Dave and Gary were having a great time. They were attempting to play Ping-Pong with no knowledge of the game at all. It was the happiest I've seen Gary and Dave.

Another interesting thing was what happened this afternoon with Pete. While playing pool with us, he turned his attention to the TV which just happened to be on. A news bulletin concerning Vietnam came on, and before I knew it, he was into telling me how his brother was coming home from Vietnam in a few days and how he was looking forward to his arrival. In addition, we found out that we had similar views on Vietnam. He bombarded us for about an hour concerning details of the war he never fully understood. Possibly Paul Goodman is correct when he says most of education is incidental and teachers should only be available when they are needed.

On the way back to the car, Pete said to me, "Hey man, long-haired professors are okay." I said to myself, "Thanks Pete. I needed that."

During the drive back to the school, I couldn't help but think that this is education and this is where it's at. That is, living and encountering kids in their lives outside the school. As soon as we approached the school, the cursing started concerning their regular school. Their hate for schooling was quite evident. (*School—ain't no way . . .*)

November 17

We arranged for a chartered bus and took off today with the thirty-four kids for a large cosmopolitan area outside of West Virginia. The kids began arriving early this morning with all sorts of food, candy, soda, and paper bags full of sandwiches. In addition, their parents had given them money so they could buy souvenirs when they arrived at their destination. Many of the working class Appalachian parents are noted for their permissive and indulgent child rearing practices. In some way, erratic "big" expenditures seem to be a way of showing affection to their children.

On the trip to this cosmopolitan area some kids attempted to get the whole group to sing songs but all attempts fizzled out. Most of the time on the trip the kids usually did things in small clusters or within the reference group they belonged to. One of these small groups was able to sing to the end "One Hundred Bottles of Beer on the Wall." I also saw sadness on the faces of those few kids who didn't have a reference group. They sat silent and they stared either out of the window or into space. This type of behavior and the failure of our Boiler Room School community meetings indicated to me that we still did not have the group cohesiveness among the kids themselves. The individual seems much happier when he's in a role of participant in a small reference group. Often when we gave a child a leadership role, he would fall back into a follower-participant role and would seem to care less about the accomplishment of group goals.

While I was reflecting on these thoughts, I noticed that Ben and Jerry were sitting in the back of the bus among the kids and Jack and Jane were sitting up front away from the kids. I had the feeling that Jack and Jane were having second thoughts about the program. Jane, of late, seemed to be quite uptight and any time a kid reached out and touched her she would cringe. She was constantly screaming at the kids when they did not do something or behave properly. Perhaps she's finding out there is more to teaching than wanting to help the "poor little children of Appalachia."

There is more involved than just wanting a challenging job. In many respects, except for some knowledge in art, she had very little to offer these kids who really wanted to know so desperately about life. I think this feeling was quite evident to the children who were constantly testing her. A good example of this was in the way Gary and Pete sat in back of her and constantly kept talking about "fucking and screwing" until she blew her cool. She turned around and called them "animals." I felt after this that they were saying to her, "We knew you felt this way and we wanted you to say it out loud." Her challenge was also the kids' challenge to bring forth the true feelings she had for them. Similarly,

Jack was also having the same difficulty but to a different degree. Precisely, he told me that when he was in the army he didn't like the "mickey-mouse" details and the imposed discipline. However, at the same time he hadn't realized that many times he imposed these structures upon the kids. He was constantly imposing "punishment" of no talking in his learning center or yelling when kids were not paying attention to him. On the other hand, he was starting to see the inconsistency between his beliefs and his actions, while Jane could not.

Up to this point, I felt Ben and Jerry had grown most through their experience in the Boiler Room School. Once they were able to forget about imposing their middle-class values and once they were able to stop playing teacher, they were ready to encounter these children as real persons. I felt they were rediscovering their Appalachian culture. On many Saturdays, they would take some of the kids hunting or fishing with them, which also got them into the homes and lives of our kids outside of the school.

Once we got to our destination, we first went to a museum. Their exhibits were composed of anything from dinosaurs to a model of a coal mine. The only thing I asked the children to do was to become involved with as many exhibits as they wanted. We would be with them in order to answer any questions they might have. Some of the teachers felt the children needed more guidelines because they might destroy the place. I felt it was about time we started to trust them and this was an opportunity for them to start making choices. Some got involved with the exhibits and asked questions of myself and other teachers. They also questioned the museum directors or guides, while others just roamed around and rode the elevators, which also was just as useful. They must have time to "fool around" with the environment before they start making choices of what interests them. Many of the kids who feared elevators before were just fascinated by them. In fact, we couldn't get some of the kids off until it was time to go.

We left the museum and went to a planetarium, which upon our arrival we found out was not going to open for another hour. In the meantime what were we going to do? I decided it might be fun just to let them "fool around" in front of the planetarium. There was a huge fountain which was spurting water into a large pond. Around this fountain were benches and trees. The kids were enthralled with the fountain and pool. Some ran through the spurting water while others were pushed in. I don't believe this fountain has ever gotten better use than today. The people in the office building which overlooked the park were standing at the windows with a look of "what the hell is going on." I believe many of our museums and parks could be used better as above, instead of treating them as we treat cemeteries.

Before I knew it the planetarium had opened, and as was the museum, it was an exciting adventure. The kids were just flabbergasted with models and exhibits, especially the one where by pushing a button a brief piece of information came out about the model. In turn many of the models would operate in accordance with the information being given. The most beautiful part of this day was a film we saw in a 360° theater. Our kids just couldn't refrain from talking during the showing of the film. There was also another group of kids attending the show and they were from a suburban area outside the city; supposedly their school was a brand new open space school. What amazed me was that they were lined up outside the planetarium and marched in single file and seemed to be well dressed and well schooled. Before the film started some of these kids had asked me who were these funny kids I was with. "Are they hillbillies?" "That's what our teachers told us." They will probably be the ones who, in between their trips to Florida or skiing trips in Colorado, will ask someone like me, "What can we do to help the 'poor people in Appalachia?'"

During the film, Ted Williams sat next to me. When about ten minutes had passed, he started to compliment the dialogue of the movie. He told me about matter, anti-matter, electrons, protons, Pluto and the galaxies. How could a child who supposedly cannot read, learn about such things? I asked him. He told me that whenever there was a TV program on science, science fiction, space shots, or NASA, he would sit and watch because of his interest in the stars. The sad part of all this is that for seven years he has been classified as a Special Education student and was considered by many teachers as hopeless. Nevertheless, I'm excited, for now we have an interest and we may be able to integrate the learning of his deficient skills around his interest of the solar system. This discovery of Ted Williams's interest makes it all worthwhile.

On the way home the kids were quite restless; they had to release a great deal of emotional and physical energy which they were used to doing in late afternoon. When we arrived at the school, the buses had left, so each teacher took a group of students home.

I have a good feeling about today and I think the

more we can keep these kids away from that prison they call a school, the better off they will be.

November 22

Almost half the class was absent because it was the beginning of deer hunting season. In Appalachia everything seems to stop for the beginning of the deer hunting season. The Appalachian person puts off doctor's appointments, community meetings, household chores, etc., in order to hunt. It gives him an opportunity to forget about his troubles and to be with nature for awhile and to release his pent-up adventure seeking behaviors in his forests and hills. It gives him an opportunity to revert back to the frontiership of his early ancestors.

When the Appalachian is hunting, he feels he is serving nature. He feels in hunting certain animals that he and his prey are cooperating with nature in a sacred activity—one of the few experiences in the Appalachian's life where he is in complete control of his actions.

The kids who were in school today were involved in such activities as working math puzzles, playing Password, weaving, and playing Monopoly or checkers. Some kids who hadn't had an opportunity to work on the motor were now working on it this afternoon; the complete motor gang was absent. Ted Williams spent all day developing his solar system out of styrofoam balls and wire. We couldn't supply him with enough materials to quench his thirst for the knowledge of the solar system. Alongside Ted were some other kids who were putting together models of parts of the body, while also learning about the functions of these parts. In addition,

Nancy and Betty who still could not get involved with any one area of interest began a newspaper. They were early maturers, in the physical sense and needed attention of the opposite sex. The paper presented them an opportunity to do this by interviewing many different boys in our program. This was especially good for Betty as her mother was divorced three times and seemed to lack any love and caring for by a male figure. Many people in the school consider these girls whores, but it was not true. They wanted to find someone who would marry them in order to escape their lives at home. It is interesting to note that once the Appalachian girl gets married she takes much of the responsibility of running the household. Usually, she has more education than her husband and is more skilled in social interactions than her husband. I just observed this in an accountant's office where the husband spoke to his wife and she in turn spoke to the accountant regarding their financial matters. In short, the Appalachian, outside of disciplining, is matriarchal in nature. The father usually shuns social activities and feels his major goal is to provide the money for the family to exist on.

Both Nancy and Betty think this is the way it should be and that if the men they married didn't slap or beat them every once in a while, they would feel their husbands didn't love them. (It seems that women's liberation would not have a chance in Appalachia.)

After a bit of arm twisting, I found a typewriter and a room so that they could put together their newspaper. The principal caught wind of the newspaper and cornered me in the hallway regarding its purpose. He felt that the teacher who was an expert in newspaper writing should look it over before it was circulated. He felt it would not be in good taste for a newspaper to have typing and grammatical errors which he felt would happen if Nancy and Betty were responsible for writing it. He could not see that I was not interested in the grammar and the typing of the newspaper, but only in giving these girls a chance to be recognized and to develop an interest without the fear of doing something wrong. After my brief encounter with the principal, I went back to the girls and helped them put it together the way they wanted to do it. The principal's remarks had faded. Another thing I found out while working with these girls was their concern about being in a dummy class. They felt all the "nice" girls with all the nice clothes weren't in it, thus, this meant something to them. I didn't argue with them. In many respects, in the eyes of the rest of the school, they were considered the misfits. Since the incident on the first day, I decided not to cover up the fact, hoping that maybe this would not matter to them before the end of the program.

This might be wishful thinking, for it is very difficult to undo in eleven weeks what has been done to them day after day for seven or eight years when they have constantly been told by either verbal or nonverbal behavior of the teachers that they're no good.

December 1

This morning I met with a parent who was concerned about the program and its effects on her children. As previously mentioned, I was not allowed to get in touch with the community; however, we were constantly asking them to come in on their own. They rarely did. My only other encounter with a parent was a phone call regarding a son staying home from school when one of his four brothers and sisters were sick, which meant he was out of school at least twice a week. I was just calling to see if I could offer some help in transporting him to school or could come to the house and tutor him. Over the phone the father mentioned to me that he didn't like people who fit one of the following three categories: that is, people who are either Yankees, or Catholic, or Italian. Needless to say, the conversation did not continue; I met all three criteria.

Thus, I was apprehensive about my meeting with the one parent who came in to see me. I really didn't know what to expect. She was in her late thirties and seemed to be somewhat overly dressed and made up. After meeting her, I felt she was as scared as I was. She began by telling me that many of the children in the program liked me and that I was treating them fairly. She also went on to say how she and many parents of the working class category were scared to go to the administration and criticize the "goins-on." She felt if they did this, the principal and teachers would take it out on their children. She mentioned that it was quite difficult for her to keep quiet when she knows many of the Appalachian children are being beaten up. Another thing she mentioned was the lack of communication between the upper or middle-class parent in the school and the working-class parent. Usually, the upper or middle class was quite vocal regarding the conditions of the school. They were constantly bickering with the school administration over the filth in the school and in the cafeteria. They could not see that one of the reasons was not because of Junie's inefficiency but because when kids are treated as animals and second-class citizens they will in turn meet these expectations.

Besides the problem of not being able to get together with upper-income parents, she started to tell me why she really came in. She had heard from some other parents that I was a psychologist and that when we went to the city that I really took the kids to a mental hospital and the kids were told not to say anything about their trip to the mental hospital. After about half an hour I convinced her this did not happen and that I was not a psychologist but only a person who wanted to learn about her culture. I think that she believed me and that some of her superstitions of me were eliminated. We agreed that next year she and any other mothers who wanted to get involved with the program would be more than welcome. She felt if they had somebody who supported them, they would be willing to stand up against some of the regular school's policies. However, she was quite skeptical concerning what she could do in our project with only an eighth grade education. I told her she probably could do a more effective job than any other teacher because her mind was not cluttered with educational jargon. After she left, I felt at least I now had an entrance into a very suspicious and closed community.

The project's afternoon activities centered around a benefit basketball game of Iannone's Raiders vs. Booker T. Washington Youth Center. The proceeds from the game were to be used for the bills I have accumulated over the last ten weeks. Some of the kids were working on how to set up a concession stand, some were working on learning how to video tape the game, some on announcing the game, and some were working on advertisements and making posters. Betty and Nancy were the cheerleaders and they were practicing their cheers. I felt this was great for Betty and Nancy.

Another interesting event today was my encounter with Gene. He was always full of life and when he did something, he did it with all he had. He liked working with Lisa, who was his girl friend whom he hoped to marry. They worked great together. In addition, he was very aggressive and loved to punch just for the fun of it. It was easy for me to talk to him, which I think really helped to add to a very close friendship. This afternoon I noticed he was trying to avoid me and he kept hiding his face. When I was able to sit down and talk to him today, I noticed his whole face was red as a beet. After some coaxing, he proceeded to tell me that the temperature had dropped near zero the previous night and that it got very cold in his house. He said it only had a coal stove in the middle of the living room and that their bedrooms were freezing. His brothers and sisters gathered around the stove to keep warm and they fell asleep. When he awoke, he noticed his face was aching and burning and he received a severe case of stove burn. After he told me this, which was quite difficult for him to do, he turned away and started to look for Lisa.

After this encounter, I started to help the other teachers in their activities. They were using old standardized tests which we found in the storage room. We had found them quite useful for helping our kids increase their reading and mathematics skills. They worked better as teaching aids than using them according to their original purposes. I guess we all realize that testing is a "bust," especially for these children.

While I was working with some of the kids with the

standardized tests, Jack approached me and told me that Pete just threw a piston at him. However, he said he got himself away from the situation because he would have hit Pete for sure. I know how difficult this must have been for Jack and I felt good about the way he handled it. Pete told me later on during the day, he couldn't take Jack any longer because he was constantly acting like a sergeant in the army and he hates to be pushed around so he started to work with Jane and he seemed to be quite happy. He did some beautiful paintings today. Perhaps, it's Jane's femininity that attracts him to her. Whatever it is, it seems to work wonders for Pete, especially after the piston throwing incident.

One final note about today. Gary and Dave are still floundering. Except for occasional interests in leather work and math puzzles, they still have not found themselves or their interests. At least they seem to be happy, which is something that didn't happen to them in the regular school.

As I was talking to Dave about his first grade experiences since he felt this is where he started to hate school, he said, "I started to hate 'book learnin' three or four years ago in first grade." This is impossible for he was presently in the ninth grade and some nine years have passed since he was in the first grade. Nevertheless, for Dave the conception of time was not as important as where he was going to get drunk that night. He lives from day to day and never worries about what happened yesterday or what is going to happen tomorrow. Today is the primary concern and how he can best survive it, just the opposite of what present schooling in Appalachia provides.

December 3

The basketball game which took place last night was a financial success and we made enough money to pay off some of my debts. We got slaughtered 73 to 40. Really, I could care less about the final score; what was important was that the kids were finally functioning as a group or community in the process of organizing their basketball game. The side effects or latent functions of this were most important regarding their learning. Specifically, some learned how to write and spell by making posters, some learned math by giving out correct change and some learned how to put ideas together by announcing the play by play of the game and others learned the mechanics of using the video tape machine. This basketball game and its related activities were most important in making real the learning of basic skills which these kids will need in order to survive in Appalachia. It's ironical that many school people realize the importance of such projects for when students work as a community in organizing either a play or musical program or athletic event they learn more than attending the typical paralyzing classes of today's schools. Yet these projects are usually perceived by school people as only interludes to the hum-drum of schooling.

Today, a safety officer came in and talked to those who were interested in hunting, fishing, and trapping. He also had a display of many different types of guns and shells that were used in hunting. The kids were enthralled by the officer and his knowledge. It lasted for three hours and for all three hours he was bombarded by all sorts of questions.

For a good part of the day, I worked with Chris and Ida, who had a very low opinion of themselves because of their inability with the basic skills of reading and writing. Previously, I had worked with them with comic books. The results were surprising, especially when they had the pictures to go along with the words. Usually comic books are more interesting than the traditional reading books. These kids had liked the comic books that had love stories. Today, they didn't want to work with comic books, but wanted to find out how to order something from a Sears or a Montgomery Ward catalogue. We went over how to fill out the order blank and how to work out the total sum for their purchases. It helped them with reading and ordering and also helped them with grasping some basic skills of adding and subtracting. By the end of our session, they were able to order and figure with very few mistakes. It was a gratifying experience.

Another girl in our program, Mary, approached me near the end of school and told me she wanted to commit suicide. Her father doesn't live with her mother but comes home when he gets the sexual urge. She told me that on one occasion her father raped her which has caused her mother to be jealous of her. On top of it all, her mother is a diabetic and can't do very much for herself or the rest of the family so Mary has to take over after school and on weekends. She pointed to her forehead and showed me some scratches and said that they were razor cuts from attempting suicide a couple of days ago. Right at this moment, we were interrupted by the principal and she left to take her bus. As she left, I told her to call me or anyone else if she felt like doing something like that again. Perhaps, now that many of the kids in the project are taking the responsibility for their own learning, we will have more opportunity to work with the Marys, Petes, and Bettys. Jane called tonight and told me that Mary had called and just wanted to talk to her. I thought this might be good for both Mary and Jane. They both may find out about each other's perceptions and values. I don't think Mary will really commit suicide. I intuitively feel that she wants the attention of someone and Jane may fill this need or void.

December 7

Our last week!

It starts off by everybody being forced to stay in their rooms for no apparent reason. What the hell was the principal doing today? No one knows!

Lou Taylor was here today for the first time in two weeks. He liked to build models, so we gave him a model car to build and one of the teachers sat down with him in order to help him read the directions. He was completely illiterate and his constant absences didn't help in building any skills. We would be getting just to a point with him where he felt confident in attempting to read or write when he would be gone for a week or two because one of his younger brothers or sisters was sick. His mother and father had a superstition that something would happen if all the school-age children did not attend together.

Billie and Scott were about the most intelligent kids in the group and they spent the whole afternoon on the roof of the school building a weather station. After building their weather station, they spent the rest of the afternoon giving weather reports to anyone who asked them about what they were doing. Previous to this project they had written a story which was quite creative. They told me that the next project after learning about weather was to prove to me that the theory of evolution was heresy. Billie was quite articulate regarding religious concepts. He felt he had learned a great deal from his father, who was a self-appointed minister, and someday he hoped to be one also.

Many of the parents of the kids in the project are irreligious and except for praying to God when they need something, they usually don't attend church. When they do attend, their praying takes place in a "good" revival service with a screaming evangelist, singing, guitar playing, and praying out loud. Traditional orders of ministers are suspect, thus anyone that feels he has the word of God, appoints himself as a minister as Billie's father did.

After school, we had a meeting with the principal and his staff (three out of his eleven staff members showed up for the meeting) to assess the progress of the program and determine whether or not it would continue next year.

The meeting was a total failure. The principal's ineptness and his staff's dissatisfaction were readily apparent throughout the meeting. It was sort of sad because I really liked him as a person. I also thought a great deal of him because he was the only principal in the county to let the program into his school. Even so, he was a good illustration of the "Peter Principle" at work. That is, as a principal he was completely incompetent, but it has been said that he was an outstanding physical education teacher. Thus, because of his ineptness the faculty of the school was broken into factions, each one trying to destroy the other by the typical backbiting which takes place in all schools. It was ironical because during the meeting he was telling me how a school faculty should function in order to accomplish its mission. What is even more depressing is that his incompetency and the lack of cohesiveness among the faculty is affecting the three hundred to four hundred children of the school. Often he would say things that he didn't mean, usually causing a great deal of consternation among the people he was talking to.

At one point during our meeting, he turned to one of the Boiler Room teachers and said, "I would never hire you because I don't know whether or not you could teach and control a regular classroom. One thing I look for when I hire a teacher is not his or her ability to teach, but how well he or she controls the children." He also went on to state that our program is not like the regular classroom because a school could not function efficiently using our alternative learning environment. His inarticulateness and criticism of our program got so bad that two of the project teachers left the meeting.

After his exhibition of ineptness in running a faculty meeting, the principal spent an hour with me explaining that he really didn't mean it the way it sounded in the meeting. You know what? I really don't know what he meant. All I know is that the man is oblivious to his failings and to what is happening to the staff and the program in his school. Presently, the major portion of his time is spent disciplining or looking for kids who are skipping their classes and hiding in the woods or in the crawl way under the school.

(*School—ain't no way . . .*)

December 8

I was the first one to get there this morning. Each teacher came in separately and one by one they sat down and did not say a word. Then Jerry came in, and before he sat down he ran out throwing up his breakfast along the way. Probably, it was how everyone felt at that moment.

After Jerry returned, we attempted to talk about the meeting, but it was no use. I could see they were physically and mentally beat. In many respects, I got the feeling they wanted to cop out even though we had only two days to go. Once we were able to get our feelings on the table, we decided that it was not only the principal, for he was just a victim of a very sick system. In fact, he is the fallout of a system that has a terminal disease. He is one of the built-in mechanisms of the public school system that destroy anything that is considered heresy or deviates from the norms of schooling. While reaching this conclusion, we felt that since the kids and their progress were most important, we could cope with him for another two days. We were convinced that our kids had developed a sense of self and were beginning to sense who they were and were developing some sort of control over their learning. These kids had feelings we could not measure, but in the last three weeks we noticed the kids were uplifted in their self-concept and sense of being. These results gave us the fortitude to stick it out for at least two more days.

During the afternoon activities, the kids confirmed the feelings we had earlier and we were now glad we hadn't copped out. Today, Jane had some of the kids make drawings out of tissue and the results were great. In addition, the Motor Pool Gang chopped down some trees and built a tripod to help them slip the motor back into the car. They borrowed a chain from Junie and the newly painted red and blue engine was jockeyed into the motor mount. All the consternation with the principal was well worthwhile just to see the look of ecstasy on the faces of the boys in the Motor Pool Gang when they finished hooking up the motor and got it to start when they were through. After a while, they ran down the battery; however, I could sense the feeling of self-confidence and pride these kids had. This type of success and many more of the same were needed by these children.

It's unfair to leave these children after we have brought them so far. Perhaps, I can get permission to continue the program next semester with another group of prospective teachers. Tomorrow, I will find out from the principal whether or not he'll allow me to continue the program.

December 10

Last day!

All shit broke loose! The screaming, shouting, fighting, and swearing that was present the first day was also evident today!

We attempted to give some standardized tests to them to see if over these last eleven weeks some learning in the traditional sense of the word had taken place. Some of the kids took these tests, while others refused to.

After our testing period, we attempted to have a small party. It was a total flop. Betty and Nancy were running around the industrial arts room where the party was taking place. They were showing everyone an article that appeared in one of the local papers explaining the details of the project. In the article, the words "slow learners" were used. This was all they needed! They kept running around the work benches yelling, "We are dummies and retards." "We are dummies and retards."

Very few of the kids paid attention to them; however, the commotion was increased and it was crazy, wild, and unbearable. Besides, Pete and Betty got into a slapping and kicking battle. This was not supposed to end this way. Good-byes should be a time when friends show other people how much they care and love them. The climate of this room was everything but this.

Midway through the display of anger and frustration by the kids, I felt maybe it was the only way they knew how to tell us that they were upset about our leaving. Even though I told them that I would probably be back the following semester with another group of prospective teachers, they refused to believe me. I couldn't blame them. Since their parents and ancestors have been exploited by coal operators, lumber companies, and local politicians over the last fifty years, they have become suspicious of anyone that only lives with them for a short period of time. This was best represented by what Pete said to me as I was explaining to them that I would be back in about six weeks and then we could start off from where we left off. Pete's response to this was, while pointing to his heart said, "I give some of this and what happens, you leave me." "Bullshit."

December 18

I had a meeting with the principal of the school and the superintendent for secondary education and received approval to have the program next semester. The principal wanted me to implement some modifications which I agreed to because I knew his inefficiency was the best thing we had going for us in this program. Generally, his comments were related to the aspect of controlling the children better. I would have agreed to anything at this point, for I didn't want the children to feel that I was leaving them to be mangled by the regular school system. In addition, I knew I was quite skillful in being subversive. That is, this past semester I learned many different ways of keeping the principal happy while at the same time allowing the children to move about freely in the project areas. On many occasions I had used his own power to defeat him. I really could care less about the principal's demands at this time. I just wanted him to take back a message to the kids that the program was still on for next semester.

One final note, the superintendent seemed very supportive of me. He convinced the principal to release some of his funds (in the neighborhood of $300) so I could buy more materials for the Boiler Room project.

I felt ecstatic after this meeting because the last meeting with the kids and Pete's comments were still very fresh in my mind. I didn't want their pessimistic or fatalistic attitude about themselves and the world they lived in to be reinforced by my not coming back next semester.

Interim

I spent the Christmas holidays in bed with pneumonia and a touch of mononucleosis. Jack had developed an ulcer and also came down with mononucleosis. Jane had received an offer to teach beginning in January. Jerry had switched from education to the field of guidance and counseling. I don't know what happened to Ben. At this writing, Bill is traveling around the country trying to get his head straight.

I wondered whether or not we were victims of "Culture Shock." That is, the results of being in a culture that is totally foreign to you. Perhaps, because we were totally unaware of the Appalachian culture and by becoming conscious of it, we were overcome by it. Similarly, I think it's the same kind of culture shock the Appalachian person goes through when he moves from a small hollow to a large city like Chicago or Detroit.

It may be that we were not only victims of culture shock, but also victims of the *"School—ain't no way . . ."* syndrome. In short, while adjusting to this new culture, we were also having our stamina and spirits broken many times by the regular school system, squelching our deviation from its one dimensionality. Even though we might have been beaten to some extent, both physically and emotionally, I'm looking forward to getting with the kids again. You might say I have fallen in love with them and have developed an Appalachian consciousness. I feel this love is stronger than anything the school system can impose upon me.

January 20

Bob and I drove out to the school to check on whether or not there had been any change in plans for the program to start in the beginning of February. When we got out of the car in the parking area in front of the school, I noticed Pete, Gary, and Dave staring out of the industrial arts room as prisoners look out throught the steel bars of their cells. As we came closer to the front door, they gave me the peace sign. I read their lips in which they asked me if I was still coming back this year. I nodded affirmatively.

Once inside the school, memories flashed across my mind about last year. This didn't last long. I could hear the gym teacher yelling at a student something like, "No. No. No. You're supposed to jump not skip."

The principal was on his way to teach a class because I guess they just did not have enough teachers in mathematics to satisfy the academic-oriented-minded parents of the community. Therefore, because of not enough funds, he was attempting to teach mathematics.

In a very nonchalant manner, he related to me how he hadn't talked to his staff about the program. It had slipped his mind. He never told me whether or not the kids were aware of my desire to get back this semester. Nevertheless, he mentioned that at his staff meeting tonight he would see how they felt and he would have Betty call me to give me the results. I sort of felt scared and ambivalent because I thought we already had agreed upon running the program this semester and I felt maybe the principal was having second thoughts.

When Betty called tonight she told me about the faculty meeting and its results. In short, she said if I would keep the kids locked up for three and a half hours in the afternoon, I would have their permission to run the program. She related that some of the teachers were pissed off because kids like Gary, Pete, and Dave and others were worse in the classrooms than before they entered our program. They could not see that their rebellious attitude was a result of their newfound sense of self. In other words, they could see that these boys were each saying to the system, "I'm going to fight you as long as you keep trying to destroy my identity."

After Betty's phone call, I did a great deal of introspection and came to the conclusion, I could almost agree to anything, but to literally lock them up for three and a half hours is too much to expect of five prospective teachers and me. The kids are better off roaming the halls, disrupting classes, etc., instead of being caged up like animals. Perhaps, I'm rationalizing my decision not to go through with the program for this semester. It could be the thoughts of watching five prospective teachers go through the phases of culture shock. It could be that the thought of constantly being harassed by both teachers and the principal day after day is unbearable. It could be the thoughts of being allowed to work in a certain box, but as soon as I stick my head out of this box, it's slapped down again. Possibly, I just was too mentally and physically tired to cope with the kinds of constraints and restrictions that were imposed upon me last semester.

I'm "copping out." (*School—ain't no way . . .*)

"This world would be a lot better off without fences . . .
people could be more free."

"Hey man, a general store!
Ah, you wouldn't know what I mean,

It feels so good to be in there,
drinking cokes!"

"Man, walking down country roads!
those ol' lonesome roads
dusty roads
kicking stones
drinking cokes
breaking bottles.
It feels so good!"

Wayne Houser, 15

from *Noris* Arts Project, 1969
Knoxville, Tennessee

What will happen to the Boiler Room kids now? The majority of them will probably drop out at sixteen and marry. They'll carve out a life for themselves in some small hollow in northern Appalachia. There might be some who have the courage to leave the mountains and seek jobs in cities like New York or Chicago. However, in many cases after about three or four years in these cities, they'll return to the mountains where they are most secure and happy.

I feel that we were successful in discovering some of their interests and in helping them to learn more about things which interested them. We were also successful in getting them to articulate more than they had previously done in school. Learning experiences centered around the following: crafts using leather, burlap, stitchery, stone, paint, carpentry, motor building, and terrarium building; other materials such as ESS and SICS science materials, Cuisenaire rods, math and language games and puzzles (*Big Rock Candy Mountain* magazine is full of ideas for games and puzzles), comic books, cheap paperbacks, model building, video tape recording, Appalachian studies materials, catalogues, magazines, encyclopedias, Play Doh, Tinker Toys, and others too numerous to mention were developed to meet the individual's interest on the spot. It is interesting to note that many of these learning experiences were sensory in nature.

I offer a word of caution here. The reader must not assume that if a teacher uses these experiences in the classroom that automatically the problem of schooling is solved—ain't no way.

The important part of this experience was not the learning experiences but the attitude we developed in working with the kids, the trust and respect developed among ourselves and the children. When we became ourselves and not teachers, the child and the situation defined the learning experience which was to be used. Our open-ended school did not exist in the finite number of learning packages or learning centers we had developed but was what existed in our heads and this was related to how we felt about the kids, learning, culture, and life itself.

Presently, many teachers may think that the experiences mentioned above and throughout the story are quite fashionable and thus be seduced into jumping on the bandwagon of open-ended education. When this is done these experiences will be killed off just as was activity curriculum, behavioral objectives, team teaching, nongradeness, sensitivity training, modular scheduling, etc. It is not the idea or technique that is important but the process and attitude of those people involved in schooling. Unless this is realized, these experiences become ends in themselves and only become newer and a more fashionable dressing for present schooling; hence they would perpetuate the same attitudes that now prevail in our schools—competition, alienation, aggression, boredom, etc.

I feel that our experiences and struggles with the kids were successful but the battle was lost within the political and social realities of the situation. For example, the majority of my time during the Boiler Room program was spent encountering regular teachers and administrators, warding off their trivial complaints and harassment. It was to these external forces which we lost our battle and to our own shortcomings in knowledge of survival tactics and risk-takings. It will be in these areas that the battle or struggle for creating more humane and alternative learning environments will be won or lost and it is exactly these points that I will discuss in the latter sections of this book.

I honestly feel that these children are much better off by dropping out of school instead of staying in. Presently, the realities of the public school system in Appalachia are such that it is an anathema to their culture. Just as the coal and lumber companies raped their soil and forests, respectively, the public school system in Appalachia is trying to rape them of their culture and soul. This is not only true in Appalachia but throughout the school systems of America. It would be redundant to repeat what has already been said about the American public school system by such cogent writers as John Holt, Jonathan Kozol, Charles Silberman, Herbert Kohl, and many more. On the other hand, it seems appropriate to mention the fact that *School—ain't no way . . .* consists of forcing the child to conform to the "School's consciousness" which includes the values, customs, traditions and beliefs of the middle class. And if the child deviates from this consciousness, he will be brought back on course by the rewards and sanctions of teachers and administrators. Ivan Illich calls this imposing of the school's consciousness upon students "the hidden curriculum." Whatever one may call it, it is still evident that this is happening to students day after day and except for some Band-Aid solutions being offered to solve the schooling process, it is in some way or another destroying sixty million children a year. Time after time it was proven to me that the regular schooling process "ain't going to work" for the Appalachian child or in fact any of the children across America. Looking back over these eleven weeks, I felt at times we didn't have the right kind of skills to help them carve out a better life for themselves in the Appalachian culture. That is in such areas as carpentry, mechanics, plumbing, masonry, environmental control, machinists, reclamation, community or citizen action organizations, labor organizations, effective hunting or fishing practices, flood control, and many more areas which could help them to keep their culture intact while at the same time developing skills that might help gain control over their lives. Personally, I don't have these skills, but I hope, in the remaining parts of this book, to develop an alternative whereby these skills can be readily accessible to them.

Once the Appalachian person develops some of these skills, he may be better prepared to live in our technological world than the majority of Americans. Jack Weller states that: "... the mountaineer has not had drilled into him the virtue of working for the sake of work. He can sit on his front porch swing and be content, not having to be doing something or creating something.... When that time comes fully upon us, when machines take the task out of work, when long hours are not required for life's main strength, the mountaineer may be ready to move into the situation more easily than the rest of us...."* Some of the characteristics I observed regarding the Appalachian child tend to support this thesis. These characteristics revolved around the Appalachian's individualistic nature, his action or adventure seeking behavior, his rejection of materialism, his sincere concern for personal feelings, his

---

*Jack Weller, *Yesterday's People* (Lexington: University of Kentucky Press, 1966), p. 160.

strong allegiances to his family, his lack of concern for job satisfaction and job security, his refusal to accept leadership positions, his strong attachment to reference groups, his noncommunicative behavior, the tendency in the family structure to be matriarchal, his suspicions and fear of the outside world, his fatalistic and present orientation, and his view of education as "just puttin' in time." (Obviously not all the children we worked with in the Boiler Room project had all of these characteristics. Nevertheless, there existed more than enough commonalities among the children to help me in developing a consciousness of the Appalachian and his culture.) One could argue at great lengths about which of these characteristics are better to have and which are better eliminated. What is important is that those characteristics such as being fatalistic, the Appalachian's view of education, and his noncommunicative behavior were the types of behaviors developed by the Appalachian to cope with the rigors of the mountain environment and later with the callous treatment of "robber baron" coal and timber companies. It is in regard to these points that I strongly disagree with Jack Weller's description of the Appalachian person. He seems to imply that the Appalachian is a "poor old boy" who just can't do anything about his life. I will address myself, in the last portion of this book, to problems surrounding Weller's and my areas of disagreement. Yet, I'm convinced that the strong characteristics heavily outweigh the weak characteristics. I find myself totally immersed in a new mind-set about Appalachia. More precisely the characteristics of the Appalachian children and their elders are apocalyptical and they may be able to help the rest of us cope with the social upheaval taking place in America today.

> ... today's student plays the role of a passive receiver until given the cue to give feedback to the transmitter. The teacher who is the transmitter is perceived by the student as the authority figure with devices at his hand that will bring the student back to the norms of the institution. He must constantly manifest behavior that represents the collective consciousness of society. For example, he learns that he must obey rules, that he must respect authority, that competition is good, that teaching is the only way to instruct, that the more schooling you have the better the person you will be, and that the American way of life is the best way of life.
>
> Alternatives to the Coming Death of Schooling

****

III. Consuming, Schooling, and Babbling

While working-class Appalachians and his children are being forced to accept a culture which is foreign to them by the "immigration process" called schooling, his brothers and sisters in the large cosmopolitan areas of Appalachia and throughout America are being conditioned to accept materialism and passivity.

Much of the individual's daily life in mainstream

society programs his increasing passivity and his servitude to technology. He awakens to an alarm clock which is scheduled according to the time he has to arrive at work. The route he takes to work has been planned by the road commission, and once he reaches work, his day is scheduled according to his business appointments or production schedule. When he gets home, which depends on the amount of traffic, he eats supper in accordance with his TV habits, which usually consist of sitting in front of the TV until he goes to bed, hoping maybe the programs will get better, but they never do. He attempts to find security in the womb of the TV which really increases his alienation between himself and the world he lives in. This routine is repeated until the individual becomes a walking automaton.

In juxtaposition to programmed passivity the individual attempts to find his soul in clothes, automobiles, hi-fi sets, colonial homes, and color TV sets. His values are programmed by the media of TV, radio, magazines, newspapers, movies, etc. What he buys is largely determined by the decision made by the megamachine of big business and what they are determined to promote and sell at a particular time. The individual demands what he has learned to demand by the advertising techniques of big business from bell-bottomed pants to automobiles. This can be easily detected by a close examination of the magazines usually found today in the American household. Under the guise of helping people adjust to today's world, they condition the individual to think that the *good life* can be found by struggling each day to obtain more material possessions.

"Thus, Walter and Gloria work hard to pay for their good life and the spacious home they enjoy so much.

For Walter, this means a 12-hour day from door to door to which he willingly submits. For Gloria, this means her part-time job in the obstetrics unit at nearby Prince William Hospital and continued bargain hunting. These two are used to hard work anyway but, with all their efforts, they find themselves running harder than ever these days to keep their heads above water."* Paradoxically, as the individual attempts to find his soul through the process of conspicuous consumption, he loses his soul and potency while being promised an easier and better living.

As a consequence of servitude to the megamachine of business and industry, the individual has also come to expect institutions to instantly solve his problems. The greater the dependency the institution creates for its members, the more inefficient it becomes. In many respects, the more control a large institution has over such areas as welfare, poverty programs, cultural deprivation programs, economics, education, etc., the more problems in these areas the institutions themselves seem to create. The American public has been taught to think that once a large institution takes over one of these areas or legislation is proposed in these areas, the problem has been solved. We all know this is not true. For example, it seems the more the federal government is asked to support medical programs, the more the need for hospitals is created; and so, no longer can one get home care. Similarly, the more legislation and money poured into poverty programs by the federal government, the more poverty we seem to have. The greatest

*Sidney Margolius, "Today's Families and Their Money Problems," *Family Circle*, February 1972, p. 28.

hoax of all is the Vietnam situation. The more people, personnel, and money spent for this war, the more we have of it in regards to body counts and its length.

Many of today's individuals have come to the realization that once they have achieved and possess middle-class values, they are still unhappy. Thus, we see many different groups opting for different life styles and attempting to find some culture that they will feel most comfortable in. A cultural upheaval or revitalization by many groups in America, such as the Blacks, Jews, Italians, Women's Liberators, Gay Liberators, etc., is obviously in progress. They are tired of being treated as a number and being manipulated as the crew is on one of our Apollo space ventures. Their frustrations are causing them to say "Bullshit" to the American way of life and its striving for middle-class approved values in a plastic culture—they want to keep their uniqueness. Similarly, in a silent manner, the Appalachian wants to keep his identity and for the most part has rejected the middle-class culture. They don't want to be social engineered as this writer and other so-called professors have been trying to accomplish under the guise of offering a better life for them, which meant for them to reject their culture and values and to accept the middle-class or WASP values. The Appalachian person (and many people in America) doesn't want the American dream and its payoffs. He wants to be left alone.

The process of conditioning people to accept the American way of life begins in the schools where colonization begins to take hold of individuals. Colonization brainwashes and manipulates the individual to be subject to and worshipful of the American way of life while it maintains inequalities that exist in society. Recently,

Martin Carnoy developed this point more extensively in a paper presented to the American Education Research Association. He states:

"Schools are *colonialistic* in that they attempt to maintain economic and political relationships in the society especially among those children who gain least (or lose most) from those relationships. Schools demand the most passive response from those groups in society who are the most oppressed by the economic and political system, and allow the most active participation and learning from those who are least likely to want to change. While this is logical in preserving the status quo, it is also a means of colonizing children to accept unsatisfactory roles. In its colonialistic characterization, schooling helps develop colonizer-colonized relationships between individuals and between groups in the society. It formalizes these relationships, giving them a logic that makes reasonable the unreasonable. After emancipation in 1863, for example, the continued oppression of Blacks in the United States could be rationalized by Booker T. Washington because Blacks were not as educated as Whites. He believed that Blacks should not be regarded as equal by Whites until they made themselves worthy of equality by becoming equally educated. Paulo Freire regards the colonial situation as the culture of silence. The colonial element in schooling is its attempt to silence, to rationalize the irrational and to gain acceptance for structures which are oppressive."*

*Martin Carnoy, "Education as Imperialism and Colonialism" (Paper read at American Education Research Association Annual Meeting, Chicago, April 4, 1972), pp. 5-6.

The public school institution is no different from any other institution in creating a dependency among its clients. In fact, it is easier because the public school has a captive audience as a result of compulsory attendance laws, which in turn gives them a monopoly over education. Clients are conditioned to think that education can only happen in schools with certified teachers. Thus, the clients demand what they have been programmed to demand by the public school system; especially in regards to building new schools, purchasing new curriculum programs, hiring more specialists, and hiring only certified teachers. In addition, the clients are conditioned to think that everyone needs a degree from a school in order to get ahead in this world. The public has been conditioned by a conspicuous consumption degree syndrome. They are conditioned to think that everyone in America should have a degree to get ahead in this world. As a result, each individual is attempting to get a better and higher degree than his neighbor. In turn, this causes each degree to lose its significance over the years, such as what has happened to the elementary school degree, high school degree, and more recently, with the bachelors, masters, and Ph.D. It has reached a point of diminishing returns—how far can we go beyond the Ph.D.—Postdoctorate degree?

It is interesting to examine how the public school and its clients adapt to each other under unpropitious conditions. Consider the public school must take clients it doesn't select, and the clients are forced to attend an institution not because they want to but because of the compulsory attendance requirement. The public school adaptive behavior usually takes place in the form of segregation. The deviants are placed in voc-tech schools or the "dumping track" and the well behaved are placed in both the better schools and in the "college bound track." In addition, the public school gives preferential treatment to those pupils who are "good" in grades and discipline, and who are able to follow their assigned track without causing any trouble. Paradoxically, the public school maintains social inequalities while at the same time it says it attempts to destroy them.

The clients' adaptive behavior takes many forms. One form is situational retirement; the clients are physically present but not mentally present. They go to school in a manner similar to the way old people go to the library or to the movies. Another form of adaption is rebellious adjustment; these are clients who constantly test the limits of the situation to see to what extent they can deviate from their role expectation. Still another form of adaption is the "side payment adaptation" where they continue in school because of the fringe benefits such as social activities, competition, sports, opposite sex, etc. The greater the side payments the larger the "holding power" the school has over the clients. Finally, on extreme opposite ends of the continuum of adaptive behavior is the receptive and dropout adaptive behavior.*

Usually, these adaptive mechanisms on the part of both the public school system and its clients are offshoots of the assumptions that schools are built upon. These are: 1. All subjects should be taught and learned in classes of the same length (Monday, English, forty

*Richard O. Carlson, "Behavioral Science and Education Administration," *The Sixty-third Yearbook of the National Society for the Study of Education*, vol. 63, pt. 2 (1964), pp. 262-76.

minutes; Tuesday, English, forty minutes, etc.). 2. Classes should occur at the same time each day (Monday, English, 9:15; Tuesday, English, 9:15, etc.). 3. Teachers may not spend more time than the designated period with a given class, since this would disrupt the schedule. 4. If a teacher's room is noisy, no learning is going on; if a teacher's room is quiet, learning is going on. 5. All students coming out of a given class should know the same things. 6. All teachers teaching the same subject should teach the same things. 7. The best way to set up a bunch of students for teaching purposes is by age—therefore for the purpose of the schedule all twelve year olds or eighteen year olds are alike.*

Under these conditions, teachers have become certified social thermostats. They must keep the student's aggression alive but within carefully controlled limits. They must teach students to be nice to their friends while at the same time the students must learn how to beat out their friends in regards to marks and their place on the bell curve. The teacher usually maintains the competition that underlies most of our education system. As a result, most learning that goes on in this type of tension-management system is learning how to memorize, take good notes, and develop competitive spirit. In short, the student learns how to play school; or as Ivan Illich points out, he has become schooled, which is different from education. In reality we know that much of what we have learned has been incidental. Our education is interrupted when we go to school and we really learn how to feel, love, touch, and find meaning in our

*Harold L. Hodgkinson, *Education, Interaction and Social Change* (Englewood Cliffs: Prentice-Hall, 1967), p. 67.

lives outside of schools. The only time we really learn is when we are self-motivated to grasp something like learning how to ride a bike or drive a car. Peers, parents, and friends are all teachers during our incidental learning.

On the other hand, I've realized that John Holt and other critics of our public schools offer solutions posited on the assumption that a child, when he is ready, will learn things such as reading and writing. They infer that the child, regardless of cultural background, will run to the teacher and say, "Teach me to read, I'm ready." Such critics are victims of wishful romanticism and fallacious reasoning; they contribute more to a sloppy permissiveness in schools than to significant learning on the part of students. Books which discuss free schools, such as Rasberry's Exercises, describe learning taking place in an atmosphere of hugging, jumping on waterbeds, living in domes, etc. In Leonard's term, "Education is Ecstasy."

This is pure nonsense!

The process of learning about oneself and the world we live in is frustrating and arduous, even painful at times, as well as joyful and ecstatic. Any view of learning which unduly emphasizes one aspect at the expense of the other misconstrues what learning entails and is deficient to the extent of its naivete. Learning is not all rapture and fun, nor is it all glum attention to minutia, though it frequently entails both. For example, the process of learning to ride a bicycle or learning to paint or write is not all bumps and mistakes nor is it uninterrupted success. It doesn't take place in a social vacuum either. Usually dismissed by the romantic critics are variables related to a child's community, his parents and his culture. Variables which educators must examine more closely. I believe that there is a dangerous naivete in the assumption of romantic critics that children are all alike, regardless of culture and need only the freedom to learn. Their obduracy and arrogance concerning cultural variables result in a misdirected emphasis on Band-Aid, gimmick solutions (Cuisenaire rods, open classrooms, informal curriculum, etc.). The children of Appalachia, as is true of children from other nonmainstream cultures, simply will not begin learning or tell teachers they are ready to learn until teachers understand and accept the culture of which they are a part. Our dismal record of failure with nonmainstream students will not sensibly diminish until teachers and administrators can meet their students as real people who may not want to be engineered into a middle-class mold.

It has become increasingly clear to many educators in the past few years that our almost religious attitude toward the public school system with its closeness, nonvulnerability, Band-Aid solutions, regressive tax systems, local school boards, insensitive teachers and administrators, archaic schools of education, teacher certification, and compulsory attendance, is now infested with a terminal disease and it is on a direct path to self destruction. Symptoms of the disease are easily detected on the faces of the youth in today's schools—a caricature of despair and depression as they gaze into space day after day. Visitors to a nursing home for the elderly feel this sense of despair when there is a look of hopelessness and dull resignation that death is close by. Even so, it is easy to detect the humanness of many elderly people in and outside the nursing institution by observing them, especially in stores or public places. They are constantly searching (either verbally or nonverbally) to encounter individuals as real beings. Similarly, the same observation can be made of young children. Perhaps, this is because the elderly are beginning to discover the importance of life and how much they have lost, while children are discovering each day new things about life and the adult world. In many cases, society destroys respect and curiosity about life by placing the elderly in nursing homes and the young in schools under the pretense they need institutionalization.

The disease of "blackboard paralysis" (boredom or alienation or anxiety) is caused by institutionalization and teachers are trained to perpetuate this domesticated function of schooling. The majority of teacher trainers are well versed in pompous language. They are quite proficient in talking endlessly and not really saying anything.

> And so it came to pass that in all the cities the wise men came together and said one to the other, "Come let us reason together and decide how all the children shall be taught. For surely there is much to be done if they are someday to become all wise men."
> And there were some wise men who said, "Let us make sure that all the black children and the white children learn together for that is surely the most just way to learn." But there were other wise men who said, "Surely you know that the white parents do not want the black and white children to learn together. So let us be reasonable. Let the white and black children learn separately, but let us make sure that they all have teachers who speak the truth and teach them well." But the wise men

could not agree on this problem, and their talk grew hot and angry. And many days and weeks passed.

And then some wise men said, "Let us talk of other matters. We must make sure that the teachers have all the tools they need to teach." And then some wise men complained that all the tools were made for the teachers of the white children and not for the teachers of the black children. And other wise men said that good teachers should be able to use any tools and that it would drain the treasury to make special tools. And the wise men could not agree on this problem and many weeks passed as they talked.

Outside, in the village streets, the children waited while the wise men argued. And when a child cried, "When shall we learn and how shall we learn?" one of the wise men called out sharply, "These are great problems that take time to solve. The wise men are talking. And those who know nothing should be quiet." And the children waited.

And then one of the wise men said, "We must make sure that if one of our teachers is no longer good and true he be taken away from the children." And then many wise men grew angry and cried, "How can you know when a teacher is no longer wise? Is a teacher an ox, that you use until you grow tired of his groans and wheezes and turn out to the fields to starve? We have seen no one here wise enough to say when a teacher should be taken away from children." And the wise men argued long and loud on this problem. And many weeks and months passed.

And then a wise man said, "And how shall we know what to teach our children? If a new book is made and the street hawkers shout that it will speed the learning of children, should that book be used by the teachers?" And some wise men said, "If the mothers and fathers think the book is good, then the book is good." And other wise men said that only wise men know when a book is good.

And other wise men said that the book must be used on a small group of children first. And they argued. And the children waited outside.

And many months and years passed. And the wise men grew old and hoarse. And some left, and others came to take their place. And still they argued. And the questions were always the same. How shall the children be taught? Should there be special tools? Who is to tell when a teacher can no longer teach? Who is to decide what books shall be used? And as time passed, the noise of the wise men's voices grew louder, and soon it was as if each one talked only to himself.

And then one day, after many years had passed, there was a new noise deeper and more angry than the voices of the wise men. One of the old ones looked out of the window of the palace, and his face turned gray with fright. The children were no longer there. In their place were adults, young, strong, and furious. They held signs that said nothing for they did not know how to express themselves. They chanted slogans of hate and destruction, for they had not learned how to reason. And one by one, each frightened wise man turned to the other and said, "While we talked, they have lost their childhood. We have waited too long."*

As the above editorial so beautifully illustrates, teachers are trained within "Towers of Babble." With the possible exception of politicians, teacher educators use more pompous language, rhetoric, and heated polemics than persons in any other profession. The most depressing aspect of this is that in many cases it becomes a catechism for prospective teachers. This is manifested in mouthing such things as "individualized instruction," "democratic teaching," "human teaching," "behavioral

---

*Martin Buskin, "A Fable for Our Modern Wise Men," *Issues Today*, Teacher's Edition, vol. 2, no. 5 (November, 1969).

objectives," "interaction analysis," on and on and on goes the rhetoric. Many teachers and teacher educators alike grab onto empty phrases and spend the rest of their lives defending them, while at the same time sixty million American kids sit in submission waiting for a holiday or June so they can regain their sanity. In addition, many planners and designers of innovations in education have shown us the advantages of module scheduling, nongradedness, team-teaching, and computer-aided instruction. It is in vogue to package instruction or even emotions by use of sensitivity training or to electrify the classroom via the philosophy of McLuhanism. But what do these new techniques, processes, and innovative models have to do with the needs of today's youth? The cure that murders as it saves. Teachers and teacher educators first must contend with their fraudulence before attempting to design new techniques and processes of instruction.

Another facet of teacher education that teacher educators need to contend with is the organizational structure. Almost invariably, the present school of education structure reinforces the present public school organization. Like the public school system, the dean of the School of Education plays the role of the superintendent; the departmental chairman plays the role of the principal, the professors of teacher education play the role of teacher, and last the prospective teacher plays the role of the student. This hierarchy produces mandarins who in turn produce other mandarins so that the finished product is a teacher who is skillful in control and manipulation of children. Paradoxically, the schools of education preach the revamping of schools while at the same time they feed the school system the same "stuff" that leads it to self-destruction. Many of the causes of this destruction and the coming death of schools have been discussed by this author and other authors in various publications such as *Alternatives to the Coming Death of Schooling, Crisis in the Classroom, Death at an Early Age,* and *How Children Fail.* Similarly, schools of education are doomed. That is, like public school systems, schools of education do not adjust to outside forces and are not self-regulating organisms which are usually open, dynamic, and evolving. They protect themselves from outside forces by defensive reactions and are intolerant of conflict and ambivalence.

Any alternative or deviation from one dimensionality is considered heresy. In fact, schools of education like the public school system, become inquisitors for those who preach heresy, by making it so difficult for them to exist in the system that they eventually have to drop out.

A metamorphosis has started to infest schools of education and there is no way to stop it. Current schools of education have a terminal disease and superficial remedies such as individualized instruction, sensitivity training, behavioral objectives, etc., won't help. On the other hand, a positive aspect of the metamorphosis is that educators are beginning to question values which they had accepted blindly as truth. The very conception of truth seems to be undergoing severe scrutiny from within and from without the school system. Many believe that all knowledge is tentative and arbitrary. A generally conservative camp of educators believes learning must be hard; another camp, generally more liberal, believes "Education is Ecstasy"; I have argued that learning in any meaningful sense involves more than the single dimension these critics dwell on, particularly regarding students from nonmainstream culture backgrounds. The value of the authoritative-school-passive-learner model which has been with us so long is strongly contested by those who view the learner as essentially self-directing. Discontent is evident in every strata of society and none of it is without implication for schools.

Inevitably, teacher educators must contend not only with questioned values, but with the revolution taking place in America. Two American writers, Reich and Toffler, and a French writer, Revel, suggest that this revolution is taking place not only in technology but also in life styles and values. In many respects as the present education system is coming to an end, so is the present American era.

Some of the events referred to by these authors which teachers and teacher educators must contend with are: the emergence of three different types of nations in America; a black nation, a Woodstock nation, and a Wallace nation; a radically new approach to morals in our nation, such as the breakdown of the marriage institution, sexual freedom in the arts and among people; the search for religion other than the traditional religions found in America; an acceptance of different life styles existing within different communities causing America to become more pluralistic; women's liberators, gay liberators, black panthers, drug freaks, etc.; new approaches in international affairs such as the Vietnam pullout and the recent softening of attitudes toward Red China. Again, I must reiterate, what do the new techniques and processes in teacher education have to do with the changing nature of our educational values and of the American scene?

Moreover, many schools of education have aided the prospective teacher in becoming alienated from his profession. As Marx suggests, if the worker or consumer is not able to share in the designing of the thing he is to produce, he will become alienated. This is especially true of today's prospective teacher who is demanding more involvement in "non-education" areas such as politics, civil rights, consumer rights, and international policies, but who is not involved nor allowed to be involved to any great extent in deciding on the type of teacher education program which will meet his needs and interests. Presently, the majority of schools of education impose a teacher education curriculum system upon their prospective teachers. We in teacher education are aware of the sterility of the atmosphere we create and yet we still sit in our ivory towers and design new models, techniques, and processes to aid teachers, without examining the prospective teacher's alienation from his program. We in teacher education are institutional maintainers and help self-perpetuate the system. Our major goals in teacher education are displaced by the means which in turn become the goals. A majority of time spent by teacher educators revolves around discussion of certification, licensing, attendance, loads, credits, courses, budget, and other "maintaining" areas. Recently, Charles Silberman postulated that mindlessness characterizes today's schools, whereas he failed to mention that the same mindlessness is taking place in teacher-training institutions which engender this condition:

A school of education is preparing for an NCATE evaluation by having professors and instructors prepare behavioral objectives and syllabi for their courses. However, the goals or objectives may have little to do with what is actually taking place in the teacher education curriculum such as memorization of techniques of teaching, taking notes, taking exams, and taking methods courses which usually suppress the creativity of the prospective teachers. In many cases, when the evaluation is completed the goals are filed and the school of education will not look at them until the next accreditation which might be six years later.

A dean of a school of education was explaining that the beauty of his program was that it was individualized. What he failed to mention was that the prospective teachers were individualized by only one strategy and that was *programmed learning.*

A former doctoral student who is now a professor of education reported that his department chairman made the following regulations regarding dress for his student teachers. First, male student teachers must not wear jockey shorts under their regular pants because they are too provocative. Second, female student teachers must wear skirts that will cover their knees when they sit down. Third, student teachers must not make friends with their students, for students will take advantage of such friendships. Fourth, students must not buy beer, alcohol or toilet articles in those stores used by either their students or parents.

A colleague reported to me that during his tenure at another institution the following incident took place. A student teacher was thrown out of the program because she took part in the Kent State demonstration. However, in justifying her dismissal to his staff, the Dean insisted that he found the girl lacking in the number of days she worked in student teaching. That is, instead of the fifteen required weeks of student teaching she had only fourteen weeks and four days and did not meet the university requirements.

The federal government solicited schools of education to propose alternative elementary teacher education models and nine different schools of education were selected. Eight of the models got caught in the performance specification-behavioral objectives syndrome. The one model that was imaginative and creative and offered an exciting alternative to the present teacher education models was rejected because it did not fit the performance specification model. In addition, if one of these eight models were implemented it would consist of something like 2,000 learning experience modules, which means a prospective teacher would have to take about eight pre-post tests each day for four years.

These incidents and others reinforce the concept that not only does mindlessness take place in public schools, but that it is also quite prevalent in schools of education. Besides, many of the theories of teaching and analyses of classroom behavior, etc., stress the improvement of what already exists or continuation of the system as is. Attempting to research and analyze "in depth" something that is dead such as present schooling or classroom practices is mindlessness. This time could be spent better in examining and implementing different alternatives to schooling and teacher education.

Teacher education is a hoax. We have been sidetracked by putting all our forces in the study of teaching. Paradoxically, this is the function that helps self-perpetuate present conditions of schooling. Perhaps, we should redirect ourselves in teacher education to place our emphasis on learning instead of teaching, and to give future teachers the skills and processes that are conducive to helping each individual keep his uniqueness and his culture.

The following proposals are offered to those teacher educators and schoolmen who have the courage to use them and who are seeking new alternatives to our present obsolete teacher education practices.

1. Eliminate schools of education and replace them with training in facilitating centers which would be available to community members, businesses, parents, and students who are interested in discovering how to teach particular skills, not attitudes to individuals. Attitudes would be left to the student's encounters with the community. It could be that future teachers can guide students in their learning about the community. These types of teachers would not have to necessarily attach themselves to schools as such, but to where they are needed. A teacher may be contracted by twenty parents to teach certain skills and it would be up to the teacher to find a comfortable space for learning to take place. This may be in the teachers' or at students' homes, parks, museums, theaters, lounges, etc. It may be possible to destroy the monolithic public school system by this type of training.

2. Groups of prospective teachers can be given opportunities to start their own schools which could be proof enough of whether or not they have the "stuff" that makes good teachers. Teachers could be trained to become institutional builders as delineated in the rejected USOE Columbian Teacher Education Model. Within this type of model the teacher is given the responsibility of developing the curriculum and shaping the school.

3. Schools of education could train teachers to bring emotional support to today's youth. The prospective teacher's training experience may consist of only group encounter sessions and knowledge of child development theory. The teacher's traditional role of passing on information to today's youth is obsolete. Many other mediums such as newspapers, magazines, TV, radio, movies, records, etc., could do far better jobs in this regard. However, future teachers may be able to help today's youth struggle with their emotional "hang-ups." Thus, teachers and students can become like partners or immigrants encountering a new world both learning about each other while also learning how to cope with our Kaleidoscopic society.

4. A wider variety of experiences could be offered to prospective teachers. These experiences could be related to urban, suburban, Appalachia, Europe, Vietnam, South America, Africa, Peace Corps, VISTA, etc. That is, each prospective teacher would have the opportunity to select those experiences which best match his personality and interests. These experiences could last either a day, a weekend, a week, a month, or whatever duration might be needed to meet the needs of the prospective teacher. The individual would be given credit just by actively participating in the experiences. He might participate in a weekend workshop for learning about the British integrated curriculum or spend a month in a hippie commune learning about their life styles. The possibilities inherent in this type of matrix are plethora. In addition, many experiences may revolve around cross-cultural exchanges. That is, prospective teachers from the inner city, suburban and others, could teach in Appalachia and similarly, the prospective Appalachian

teachers could teach in these cultures. Each group of prospective teachers which are exchanged may learn how other cultures are solving and coping with their problems today, i.e., learning how ethnic politics works in urban areas and its applicabilities for the Appalachian in his struggle for survival.

5. An ad hoc arrangement may be possible for future schools of education. They may become multi-institutional in structure such that they may plug into any institution as the situation demands. They can become open training institutions or education centers without any particular alignments to a university or community. For example, it may be possible that institutions such as West Virginia University, University of Massachusetts, Columbia, and others can be combined to become an Appalachian-Urban teacher training program. A major asset of this type of setting would be the pooling of political and intellectual resources to meet the needs of people in these areas.

6. A three-year moratorium can be issued on the training of teachers. Teacher educators will then have the opportunity to have real encounters with today's youth. They will be able to match the realities of their values and interests with those of today's youth and society. Each professor of education could be offered an ultimatum. If he and his prospective teachers cannot prove their existence of his specialized area in education without being evasive, then he must start looking for those things that can support the prospective teachers' existence in today's society. On the other hand, the moratorium may never be lifted for it's conceivable that educators may decide that the community has enough resources to teach today's youth.

These proposals may help eliminate some of the problems for training teachers for the mainstream culture; however, the culturally different teacher like the Appalachian may need another kind of model than those proposed above.

Perhaps, future teachers of Appalachia and other cultures would not have to leave their communities to become teachers. They could remain in their communities while attending the university periodically to grasp the skills and resources they need for their cultural setting and finish when they felt the university could no longer help them. In other words, the culture and the community of the prospective teachers would be the core of their experiences and all other experiences, both intellectual and affective, would support this core. The university would be only one of the sources they could plug into for their experiences.

Some of the techniques and processes of the Open University in England may be adapted to fit the needs of a teacher-training model for Appalachia. Specifically applicable is the idea of a home-based university which relies heavily on self-instructional materials, radio, television, tutors, some lectures, summer schools, and brief periods spent in classes and seminars at the university.

Ultimately what must be realized by teacher educators is that they are "ripping off" the culture of the prospective teacher and replacing it with the institutional culture. Errol Hess, a teacher in Appalachia, wrote in *Mountain Life and Work* that:

> ... over half the people I went to college with are in a city somewhere, or in California and Florida. People do lose their culture in our colleges. I was made fun of by my teachers because of the

way I talked, because I was more interested in going fishing or berry-picking than going to a "tea", and because I didn't think the most important thing in life was to have my hair styled and sport a good wardrobe. I changed a lot to "fit in". I lost my accent, started wearing suits, quit going fishing, started going to cocktail parties, joined a fraternity, and learned how dumb and backward my folks were. The old song goes, "How do you keep them down on the farm, after they've seen Paree." I wasn't told in college that hillbillies have a lot of good points, that in many ways their lives are much more sane than the lives of people, say, somewhere in suburbia. I didn't learn in college that my dad had more common sense and concern for other people than the man who ran the company he worked for. I learned that "good" people sit in offices with their feet on desks, drink cocktails, and eat three dollar steaks for lunch. I learned that the common folks are wrong, worthless, and in the way of progress, and that the coal companies, oil companies and other companies have the true interest of this land at heart. "What's good for General Bullmoose is good for the U.S.A."*

*Errol Hess, "Education in the Mountains," *Mountain Life & Work*, 48, No. 4, April (1972), p. 14.

> *The reasonable man adapts himself to the world; the unreasonable man persists in trying to adapt the world to himself. Therefore all progress depends upon the unreasonable man.*
>
> G. B. Shaw

****

IV. Appalachian Consciousness of the Apocalypse

The hill or mountain person may have the concept of life that is needed to cope with our technological society. In many respects he has rejected materialism and its objective orientation of the rest of America. The Appalachian is primarily concerned with day to day life and fellowship with his neighbors. This may change in the near future because of TV, which is just now getting widely into the homes of the hill people. TV could strip them of their culture and replace it with middle-class values with an orientation toward conspicuous consumption. However, when most hill people find themselves becoming surrounded by a middle-class culture they do one of two things. They either move farther back in the hills, or stay put and reject their old culture. But, when the hill person becomes stripped of his culture and stays to pursue the American dream, he usually fails to recognize that he has a consciousness difference with mainstream consciousness. Essentially, this is the same phenomenon experienced by immigrants. For example, I am of Italian descent and I remember many times when my parents were embarrassed because of their nationality and for being forced by WASP types to "melt" into the mainstream culture or to be Americanized. This meant that the children of Italian immigrants would be named after American movie actors and actresses, who to them epitomized the true American. Specifically, instead of naming me Emilio, Mario, Giovanni, Pasquele, etc., which are Italian first names, they gave me a first name of Ronald, after Ronald Coleman. They felt this was one way of becoming Americanized. This example and many more have forced different cultures to lose their heritage and identify by processes ranging from fixing crooked noses to dyeing hair. Recently, a friend of mine, who is also of Italian descent, was hired at one of "The" liberal arts colleges on the east coast and he was given $600 beyond his salary to get specialized help in ridding himself of his New York accent with Italian overtones. He took the money, however, he donated it to a "local" chapter of the Italian Anti-Defamation League and when the institution found out, he was fired because of his incompetency in teaching.

Similarly, even though many of the Appalachians have refused to be immigrated into the mainstream culture, in turn they have become virgin territory for the large corporate companies of America.

Thus, the "gentleness" of the people in Appalachia and their lack of resistance to corporate power has become fertile ground for large corporate chemical companies such as Union Carbide and Du Pont. A specific example of these corporations and their insensitivity to the people and their land can be found in Charleston, West Virginia, which is number one in regard to the amount of pollution that is released into the air everyday by the chemical companies which have plants in Charleston. It is possible that in the next couple of years people in Charleston may be walking around with gas masks in order to protect themselves from respiratory diseases. What has happened in Appalachia is that the area has become split into two worlds, the "haves" and the "havenots," and the "havenots" have become subjects of the "haves" in Appalachia. Harry Caudill states that:

> Actually there are two Appalachias, and while they exist side by side and are jumbled together, they remain strangers to one another.
> First, there is the Appalachia of great wealth. The steep ridges are cloaked with a forest of immense age and incredible variety from which billions of dollars worth of hard and soft woods have been cut for housing, furniture, and paper. The world's best coal runs in thick veins through its hills and underlies its valleys. Limestone, talc, clays, copper, lead, iron-ore, gneiss and grahamite are only a few of the other minerals that lie above the coal beds. And far below them repose the oil and gas that the petroleum industry now regards as "very promising." This is the Appalachia of highly profitable corporations, expensive homes with swimming pools and Lincoln Continentals, purposeful entrepreneurs and beautiful and begemmed women. This Appalachia sits in the board rooms of the nation's great corporations (including Gulf Oil, Ashland Oil, Continental Oil, Occidental Oil, Ford Motors, Bethlehem Steel, United States Steel,

International Harvester, and American Electric Power), staunchly defends the profitable status quo, and denies responsibility for any of the region's woes.

. . . then there is the Appalachia of great poverty. This is the Appalachia of innumerable television documentaries and news reports. It is a land of eroded hillside farms, of mined-out and broken-down hills, flimsy shacks, roadsides lined with junked cars and trash heaps, reeking water-courses, and unwashed people who have been dependent on the dole and the relief check for decades. It is the Appalachia of dejection, despair, ill-health, and surrender.*

Most response to the second Appalachia or second variety of Appalachia has been of stop-gap or Band-Aid solution type. A great deal of "Bullshit" has been put forth in the rhetoric and pompous language of local, state, and federal politicians. However, very little has been done to change the plight of Appalachia and to help the people gain control over their lives. In many respects, we have skirted the real issues in Appalachia such as tax reforms, strip mining, exploitation by coal companies and chemical companies, and the taxing of the "super rich" of Appalachia.

Similar developments are occurring to a lesser degree in other parts of America. While we preach equality, our actions maintain the inequality that exists in today's society. Paradoxically, much of society acts like a filtration device and separates the so-called good from bad. If one is white and has a name like Smith, Curtis, Wayne, Cooper, Day, etc., and is born into an affluent

*Harry M. Caudill, *Coaltown Revisited*, by Bill Peterson, *New York Times Book Review*, May 7, 1972, p. 8.

family, he usually has a better chance of "making it" in the mainstream culture other than culturally different who are either Black, Chicano, Indian, or Appalachian. Usually these groups are filtered out by the schooling process and those children who have an affluent background have a better chance of surviving in our society than the culturally different person. Herbert Gans points out that ". . . The poorest fifth of U.S. population receives only 4 percent of the nation's annual income. . . . Although many Americans now own some stocks, 2 percent of all individual stockholders own about two-thirds of stock held by individuals. . . . Of the almost two million corporations in America one-tenth of 1 percent controls 55 percent of the total corporate assets. . . . Stein estimated the annual subsidies came to $720,000 per family for people with million dollar incomes, $650 per family for that $10,000-$15,000 middle-income group and $16 per family for the under $3,000 poor."* Egalitarianism is a myth in America.

Even though these inequities exist throughout Appalachia and America, it is interesting to note that because of this the hill person and his culture move farther back into the hollows of Appalachia. Many of them refuse to accept the American way of life and give up their freedom to a materialistic and objective oriented world. These hill people and their children are similar to what William Glasser defines as existing in a primitive identity society. Glasser posits that today's modern man has come through four different stages of development. The

*Herbert J. Gans, "The New Egalitarianism," *Saturday Review*, May 6, 1972, p. 43.

first stage is identified as the primitive survival stage where man at this stage of development is primarily concerned with just the basic survival processes of gathering food and protecting himself from the environment. The next stage is identified as the primitive identity stage where man in this stage has more free time to enjoy life and is primarily concerned with the gathering of food and sharing with his fellowman. In this stage of development he is motivated to cooperate with his fellowman and to formulate complex kinship systems. After this stage, Glasser further postulates that man went through a civilized survival stage of development where with the increase in population, the decrease of available game, and the discovery of agriculture, land became extremely valuable and aggressive men fought one another to obtain and exploit it. Presently, Glasser feels that man is in the fourth stage of development now and he identifies this as the civilized identity society stage where man has begun to move away from the collected inertia of centuries and toward a role-dominated society in which human concern again centers on self-identity, self-expression, and cooperation. This stage is quite similar to the primitive identity stage and where I feel that the Appalachian Consciousness is. The Appalachian's rejection of materialism and objectivity, his person or I-Thou orientation, his close family ties, his strong relationship to his reference groups, and his closeness to the soil both intellectually and physically seem to support this contention.

Presently, some of the hill people are still at the basic primitive survival stage, they are struggling each day to meet their basic physiological needs. These range from people who are on welfare to those that have been disabled by black lung. Thus, much of the culture at times is hygiene oriented but when some of their basic needs are met, many of the characteristics existing within the primitive identity stage are quite evident.* Perhaps, the Appalachians have been "sleepwalking" through our technological age; however, it seems that the rest of society is reaching the stage of development which the hill people have already been at since they settled in the hills. More specifically, by developing an Appalachian consciousness, I feel now that it is an injustice through schooling and the collective consciousness to force the mainstream culture upon a culture that has many beautiful apocalyptical characteristics. Their culture must be preserved. Some way must be found for the Appalachian to keep his primitive way of life without being socially engineered to accept the mainstream way of life. It is interesting to note that the "hill culture" is more similar to the new naturalism of today's youth than any other culture. They seem to meet the criteria of "new naturalism" identified by Daniel Yankelovich.

1. To place sensory experience ahead of conceptual knowledge. Check.
2. To live physically close to nature, in the open, off the land. Check. (If not destroyed by coal companies.)
3. To live in tight knit groups, rather than in such "artificial" social units as the nuclear family. Check.
4. To reject hypocrisy, "white lies", and other social offerings! Check.
5. To de-emphasize aspects of nature illuminated by science; instead, to celebrate all the

―――――――
*William Glasser, *The Identity Society* (New York: Harper & Row, 1972).

unknown, the mystical, and the mysterious elements of nature. Check.

6. To embrace the existentialist emphasis as being rather than becoming or doing or planning. Check.

7. To devalue detachment, objectivity, and non-involvement as methods for finding truth; to arrive at truth, instead, by direct experience, participation and involvement. Check.

8. To look and feel natural, hence rejecting makeup, bras, suits, ties, artificially groomed hairstyles. Check.

9. To express oneself nonverbally; to avoid literary and stylized forms of expression as artificial and unnatural; to rely on exclamations as well as silences, vibrations, and other nonverbal modes of communication. Check.

10. To reject "official and hence artificial forms of authority"; authority is to be won, it is not a matter of automatic entitlement by virtue of position or official standing. Check.

11. To reject mastery over nature. Check.

12. To dispense with organization, rationalization, and cost-effectiveness. Check.

13. To embrace self-knowledge, introspection, discovery of one's natural self. (No—Usually accomplished in regards to one's role in a reference group.)

14. To emphasize the community rather than the individual. Check.

15. To reject mores and rules that interfere with natural expression and function. Check.

16. To preserve the environment at the expense of economic growth and technology. Check. (When allowed to control it.)*

In the course of our struggling with being victims of future shock both the young of today and the hill

---

*Daniel Yankelovich, "The New Naturalism," *Saturday Review*, April 1, 1972, p. 32.

people with their naturalism can help us adapt to our "fucked up" world. The "new naturalism" of today's youth and the culture of the hill people are somewhat similar to what Charles Reich identifies as the Consciousness III person. He states that: "The foundation of Consciousness III is liberation. It comes into being the moment the individual frees himself from the automatic acceptance of the imperatives of society and the false consciousness which society imposes. For example, the individual no longer accepts unthinkingly the personal goals proposed by society; a change of personal goals is one of the first and most basic elements of Consciousness III. The meaning of liberation is that the individual is free to build his own philosophy and values, his own life style, and his own culture from a new beginning."*

Most of the writings about the "hill culture" and today's youth culture and its consciousness is usually found underground on ditto sheets, obscure magazines and journals, limited editions of small printing companies, local newspapers, etc., yet, both cultures are starting to surface together and possibly may be the consciousness of the apocalypse. This may be the Appalachian's salvation.

In the final pages of this essay, I would like to offer an alternative to the present plight of schooling and society using Appalachia as a frame of reference. At

---

*Charles A. Reich, *The Greening of America* (New York: Random House, 1970), pp. 201-2.

best, I can only offer a partial solution to the enigma of America and its social upheaval.

In regard to schooling, the Appalachian child outside of school goes to a relative or to his father to learn about such activities as hunting and fishing. He learns because it is related to the pleasure of encountering the environment and because he is interested in enjoying himself. In the primitive society, the teacher was deeply committed not only to his pupils, who were probably members of his own family, but also to the results of his teaching. If he failed to communicate his skills effectively, he felt the consequences almost at once. If a boy was not taught properly on how to hunt, his teacher might go hungry. Except for the extreme cases for "hill people" this is no longer true. However, moving this up to present day learning for survival we could see many implications of this concept. For example, if a teacher in Appalachia doesn't help his children see the ills of strip mining then the Appalachian child and the teacher may some day find themselves without the hills which are so important to them.

Today's teacher in Appalachia usually explains things that are far removed from the lives of the pupils in Appalachia. He is constantly being forced to raise his I.Q. and standard of living according to the normal population which in many respects is standardized by the rich and affluent. More specifically, the Appalachian child who is dependent and works better in concrete relationships has very little chance of surviving in today's Appalachian school because they are oriented toward abstract thinking and principles. Thus, the middle class or affluent of Appalachia usually become the leaders and the "hill people" get lost deeper into their hollows and become more suspicious of outsiders. What is needed in Appalachia and in our society is a learning system that affects the whole social order and generates conflict, confusion, tension, and frustration as man attempts to develop a new pattern of living for himself in a technological world. A tolerance for these conditions is what leads man to innovate and create designs, much like when a painter first encounters a blank canvas, he progresses through all these conditions before his painting is finished. There is a period of "controlled chaos" that one must pass through before creativity can be released. Therefore, education is learning that oneself and the world we live in and society itself are not separate entities but are in juxtaposition with each other. They must change and evolve together. To begin with, each community would become an educational system and would provide resources for young and old alike to learn skills or any specific learning desired by a person in the community. Recently, Ivan Illich said such an education system should have the following principles to guide them: Education should provide all who want to learn with access to available resources at any time in their lives; those who want to share what they know should be able to find those who want to learn it from them, and furnish all who want to present an answer to the problem with the opportunity to make his challenge known.* There could be a facilitating center in each community which could act as a museum or as a library presently does in many communities. This could be a center where a person learns skills and exchanges his

---

*Ivan Illich, *Deschooling Society* (New York: Harper & Row, 1970), p. 75.

skills with those who are interested in them. All sorts of community members could be made available to this center such as carpenters, barbers, mechanics, technologists, typists, computer technicians, etc. Computers or people could take care of cataloging skills of persons available, matching people who seek to learn a skill with another who has a similar interest and being able to retrieve information at any point during a person's learning process so the learner could assess his progress. The greatest asset of this type of learning system would be the use of people in the community as learning resources, such as senior citizens who are usually waiting in some small apartment or nursing home to die, a terrible waste of human potential. These people and their potential could be reactivated and they might start feeling again that they were active members of the community and not albatrosses around the community's neck. This is especially true of the Appalachian elderly who have a store of knowledge of folklore which has never been put down in writing but only passed on by word of mouth. In addition, in this education system there should be people available in the community who are warm, open, fuzzy, cuddly, and who can give emotional support to an individual or a group of people when they are needed. Again, many compassionate elderly people could be used in this regard. Many of us have grandmothers who could work in this role without any training at all, employing their own intuitive feelings for human beings. The resource people in this type of facilitating center would more or less act as a librarian and anthropologist in that they would guide the person to learning resources as they seek them at different times in their lives and help them release and discover their culture. Each community could take up the responsibility of training these types of directors or resource people.

An extension of this model would be similar to the functions of the 4-H agent or county extension agent who supplies the necessary skills and materials when requested by local communities in the Appalachian area. Their basic purpose is not to fit the hill people into the mainstream culture, but to help them to work out a better existence for themselves. In many cases they facilitate the "hill culture" in maintaining their independence and identity. These agents are among the few outsiders who are not viewed suspiciously by the hill culture because of what they teach about canning fruits, making soap, gardening, farming, carpentry, and many more areas which have helped the "hill people" keep their individual freedom and self-respect intact.

The illusions created by the public school system that learning must take place in schools that are taught by certified teachers can be met with negativity. School people who consist of teachers, administrators, specialists, and teacher trainers should quit their trivial and maintaining jobs in education and start examining their potential and maybe they can become what they are to become. Possibly, after teachers, superintendents, deans, etc., made a self-examination we would find an increase in the local community's number of carpenters, mechanics, plumbers, technicians and others. Once this *pull out or bankruptcy* begins we may find the elimination of teachers and their certification, compulsory attendance, school taxes, etc., the food that maintains and helps to self-perpetuate our dependency on public school institutions will be destroyed not only in Appalachia but in America.

In regard to the societal sphere, both economic and cultural resources must be given to the Appalachian. Presently, they see government as "they" or outsiders not as "we" because they have so little control over their own lives. The people that control their lives are social workers, community organizers, teachers, and politicians. These people are usually attempting to change the Appalachian to fit into the mainstream of life and its culture. In other words, when they buy something from "the man" in schools or in business, they are forced many times to also buy the man and his life style.

What must be recognized is that even though there are varying degrees of the Appalachian culture among the different hill communities, there are more commonalities than differences. They include dialects, aesthetic styles, bodies of folklore, religious beliefs and practices, political allegiances, family structures, and life styles. The Appalachian's culture is usually raped by either the mainstream culture or the "coal culture" which is built on exploitation and creating dependency on the industry. This concept is beautifully illustrated by Harry Caudill in *Night Comes to the Cumberlands.* In short, the "coal culture" uses colonialism to cultivate its subjects. West Virginia is considered a rich state. Yet it is also obvious that West Virginia is also considered a poor state. It seems that much wealth has been extracted from West Virginia's natural resources, but little of that wealth has remained in the hands of West Virginians. The reason for this, of course, lies in the exploitation of the Mountain State's resources by outside colonialism.

The Appalachian has, in many respects, had very little control over land he owns because of something called "broad form deeds." These deeds include all minerals and metallic substances and all combinations of the same, and they give the coal companies the right to remove them by any method deemed necessary or convenient. This has allowed companies to strip or surface mine land in the face of strong opposition by the landowners who had sold only the mineral rights many years before.

I feel the only way out of the Appalachian's dilemma of being forced to accept either the mainstream culture or the coal culture is to develop a bicultural democracy in Appalachia. This means that the Appalachian would be able to keep his identity and culture while at the same time having the opportunity to take whatever resources or skills he needs from the mainstream culture to help him better survive in his region. Churches, post offices, hospitals, schools, etc., should be run and operated by the people of Appalachia, not by the middle and upper class who usually defend the institutions they are working for and cannot relate to the needs of the Appalachian. In addition, large coal companies should be decentralized and control should be turned over to small business operations and local communities. The federal government should subsidize this type of operation and it should be in existence to give resources to the people of Appalachia who usually do not plan and/or design the programs that are supposed to help them. At least they wouldn't be any worse off than they were when they didn't have the resources available to them.

Probably the most important change that must take place in Appalachia and in society is the elimination of America's conspicuous consumption syndrome. This can be easily accomplished by giving to each person in America enough food, shelter and clothing to satisfy his physiological needs. With the large amount of food surplus decaying in silos and farmers being paid to keep it there is probably a good place to start. The federal government should also institute a tax reform so that the rich don't get richer because of the loopholes. A minimum sum of, say, $6,500 should be given to each person in the Appalachian area or throughout America and some controls must be available to stop price hikes when this minimum is adopted. Once this is done some people may sit around doing nothing; however, once they get over this initial period, which is part of the process of learning how to be an independent being, they would seek out those things that would help them become what they are to become. Erich Fromm stresses that ". . . Man, even under the most favorable technological conditions, has to take the responsibility of producing food, clothing, housing, and other material necessities. This means he has to work. Even if most physical labor is taken over by the machines, man still has to take part in the process of the exchange between himself and nature. . . . If man is passive in the process of production and organization, he will also be passive during his leisure time. . . ."* Precisely today the Appalachian seeks work as adventure or action-seeking and it

―――――――
*Erich Fromm, *The Revolution of Hope—Toward a Humanized Technology* (New York: Bantam Books, 1968), pp. 109-10.

must be hard and difficult. He looks forward to getting out of work so that he can enjoy himself by either getting drunk or by going hunting or fishing. In many respects, he is primarily concerned with the hygienes of his job (those things that surround the job such as working conditions, interpersonal relationships, salary, benefits, and status). He has very little opportunity to gain satisfaction from many factors that are intrinsic to his job such as achievement, recognition, responsibility, and creativity. However, the Appalachian usually finds many of these motivators in his experience with nature and if jobs were enlarged to include these motivators, more personal satisfaction could be achieved from his work. In short, we must recognize the stimuli that activate man's dissatisfaction in his work, not only in Appalachia but throughout America and we also must be able to identify the stimuli that activate his satisfactions. Frederick Heizberg and his colleagues over and over again have shown through intensified research that:

> Man tends to actualize himself in every area of his life, and his job is one of the most important areas. The conditions that surround the doing of the job cannot give him the basic satisfaction; they do not have this potentiality. It is only from the performance of a task that the individual can get the rewards that will reinforce his aspirations. It is clear that although the factors relating to the doing of the job and the factors defining the job context serve as goals for the employee the nature of the motivating qualities of the two kinds of factors are essentially different. Factors in the job context meet the needs of the individual for avoiding unpleasant situations. In contrast to this motivation by meeting avoidance needs, the job factors reward the needs of the individual to reach his aspirations. These effects on the individual can be conceptual-

ized as actuating approach rather than avoidance behavior.*

I don't want the reader to construe this to mean that everyone must be self-actualized in his job. What must be understood is that the choice or opportunity should be available to the individual if he desires it. On the other hand, if some people decide to sit around and meditate for the rest of their lives, we still would be able to function as a society; during the middle ages the monastic life was a common vocation. There may be skeptics who are concerned about the so-called sick people who could not function as independent beings. For this group, a minority of people, the Kibbutz concept would seem applicable, for this type of commune living has had fantastic results in Israel. Once the members of the Kibbutz were able to live with their independence and were able to help their children live with their independence, then they could be given the choice of staying on to live in the Kibbutz or returning to society.

A new form of citizenship and community must be developed in Appalachia so that the Appalachian can stand up and say "Bullshit" when he is encountering bullshit. A new kind of equality and citizenship must be found so that a new sense of identity can be recreated in communities where they have the power, rights, privileges, economics, and other resources to help them have a chance to live the kind of life they want to live. This is not a simple process and a great deal of dialogue

---

*Frederick Heizberg, Bernard Mausner, and Barbara Black Synderman, *The Motivation to Work* (New York: John Wiley and Sons, Inc., 1959), p. 114.

and thought must take place. The alternative for achieving this equality is not important whether it is *collective* or *individualistic* but whether or not the individual has the freedom and chance to select that alternative which makes him feel most comfortable. Peter Shrag states, "... there is a growing necessity to preserve and enlarge the place apart, to re-establish the legitimacy of the things a man can call his own; not the goods of plastic, not the future of anonymity, but the privileges of being intrinsic, the integrity of place, the ability to love and to create in the present, the gratifications of immediate expression and engagement, and the ability to live where one feels most at home."*

The Appalachian must be given an opportunity to keep his culture intact. Many of the Appalachians are spread out and live up some country road or in small hollows between two hills or mountains. There may be from two to twenty homes within a hollow. Perhaps, the "hamlet" structure of the early middle ages may be the type of community structure that could help them maintain their Thoreau-type existence while also making their needs felt on the national level. It would be possible to combine one, two, or three hollows which have close proximity to each other into one hamlet. Once the Appalachian feels that his personal goals can be met by joining forces in a hamlet, the traditional rivalries and variations in life style among hollows would be forgotten in order to achieve satisfaction of their needs. Some examples of the hollows going together have been in areas of starting a school which would meet their needs

*Peter Schrag, *The Decline of the WASP* (New York: Simon and Schuster, 1970), p. 255.

and not the needs of the mainstream culture. This type of togetherness is constantly exhibited by coal miners and their strike demands and their early militancy while in the process of organizing when they fought hard and long against the coal companies' guards. The subgroups' goals are secondary to the group coming together accomplishing its larger goals. Many of the coal mines have been shut down because of the togetherness of people from two or three hollows.

Presently, the hill people's needs are usually overshadowed by their middle-class brothers and sisters in the larger towns and cities of Appalachia. The political structure, which usually includes patronage and nepotism, is suited to the needs of the majority in these cities and towns. Thus, because of their lack of visibility and inequitable representation in state houses, hill people lose out in having their needs heard.

On the other hand, the hamlet structure may give the hill people the chance to receive the resources they need to maintain their culture through the use of advances made in technological communication.

Dr. Goldmark is a scientist who is studying new communication techniques for rural society at Fairfield University. He is attempting to discover ways to use modern communication techniques to make the rural United States more livable and more visable for having their needs met. "People must be provided with the choice of whether they wish to live and work in a large city or in a rural environment. This option does not exist today...."* He believes that the combination of

*William Smith, "A Scientist is Reborn," *New York Times*, May 7, 1972, Sec. T-5.

satellites, cable television and sound and video recording can provide rural areas education, health and political services. It seems that the rise of communication techniques and their applicability for Appalachia and other cultures are plethora.

Hamlets, through the form of debating and becoming informed, could function as the present Congress does, but in a more effective manner. If this type of structure were used for towns and cities with the invention of new communication techniques, there shouldn't be a need for Congress and our wants would directly be heard. Many interesting coalitions and cooperations among different groups would spring up from this type of arrangement. One that is quite evident in regard to its chance of happening is the possible coalition of hill people in Appalachia and the young people in asking for resources to help maintain their identity and uniqueness. Another possible example would be the "Gay liberators and hard hats" joining hands, figuratively speaking, in making their needs felt at the national level. Precisely, many "strange bedfellows" may find themselves together in their quest for culture identity. This scheme would help the federal government at the national level recognize the different cultures and their needs immediately. The Populists' needs for both economic and cultural resources could be realized by such a process instead of by an assassin's bullet.

To some extent, the concept of asking the people about their needs and then attempting to satisfy these needs seems to be the major thrust behind the recent Appalachian Movement. An illustration of this was what took place in Anmoore, West Virginia. Larry Silverman and William C. (Willy) Osborn, two young Naderites, helped a town of 900 fight the large corporation of

Union Carbide in curbing its pollution. In this small hamlet they established two main lines of action, cooperation with local individuals and groups in what they came to regard as a project in legal and community action, and intense lobbying in Washington. They helped a hamlet in grasping such skills as use of media, lobbying, citizen participation, organizing labor unions, interpreting laws, and their rights for fighting pollution.* This movement is not only made up of Nader's Raiders but many different splinter groups. Some of these are: PARC (Peoples Appalachian Research Collective) whose stated purpose is to engage in an active analysis of the political economy of Appalachia which will confront the region's colonizers, by contributing to people's movements for a democratic society.** Council of the Southern Mountains, Inc., is an older movement organization concerned with the following areas in Appalachia: Ageing, Arts and Humanities, Black Appalachians, Community Action, Health, Natural Resources, Poor People's Self-help, Welfare, *Maintaining* Life and Work, Research Youth, and Regional Economic Development. The Council is also involved with groups which have some specific purposes such as Strip Mining Abolitionists, Welfare Rights Organizations, and Miners for Democracy. Many of these groups are made up of former members or dropouts from VISTA, Peace Corps, Appalachian Volunteers, SDS, etc. Then there are the organizations like the Appalachian Regional Commission and the Appalachian Laboratory which are the arms of the federal government, and in many respects interfere with the Ap-

*Charles McCarry, *Citizen Nader* (New York: Saturday Review Press, 1972).
**"Researching Our Agenda," *Peoples' Appalachia*, II, No. 2, (Winter 1972), p. 32.

palachians' struggle for survival. The power and money of these organizations usually help to maintain the colonization of Appalachia by coal operators. These organizations and any of the anti-poverty programs seem to be also anti-movement in terms of net effect.

Nevertheless, once the movement learns the techniques of our media oriented society, and their demands and aims are known to the American public and they achieve some meaningful success, some very interesting things should take place.

Before this does take place the splinter groups of the movement must start coalescing their forces and resources and start using hamlet politics to shake the corporate power and the liberal elitist hold over Appalachia. Only when this is accomplished will the Appalachian join in. He must see some chance of success for he is not going to sacrifice his job and his family for some whimsical protest. Their militancy and their struggles in early years of union organizing were even more effective than today's Black's struggle for survival. However, at that time they were more concerned with hygiene variables such as better working conditions, higher wages and benefits. They stopped short of gaining more control over their jobs and the decision-making process in the coal companies. The only way the Appalachian movement and the movement throughout our country will be successful is when the different splinter groups within the movement can put it all together. That is, they must put their common interests above their personal goals and assault the one dimensionality of our corporate state. A leverage can be created by strategies and tactics of survival which can consist of the muckraking tactics of Jack Anderson, the clandestine operations of Daniel Ellsberg, and the perseverance of Ralph Nader. These strategies can take the form of those tactics used on the football field with some alterations. That is, these groups, whether they be research groups, labor groups, political groups, minority groups, etc., can employ different maneuvers and skirt around the *End* of the corporate state where it seems to be most vulnerable, then "hit it in the butt" until the front line defense (collective consciousness) of the institution being assaulted takes notice of its attackers and their demands. For example, exposing to public view the myths holding the bureaucratic order of the public school system together with exposing the lack of evidence to support "The Schedule" of today's school under the pretense that one is attempting to collect data to affirm its validity. Similarly, the same type tactics could be used in exposing the ineffectiveness of today's Congress.

The battle and the struggle for survival of the movement will not be won on the streets by throwing rocks and bombs, yelling obscenities, kicking and fighting policemen and national guardsmen, burning the American flag, blocking streets and offices, etc. The defense of the corporate state and its one dimensionality is just too strong for face to face physical and violent confrontation. Thus, the strategies for survival must employ the "hit in the butt" tactics or tactics similar to this until the major constituency becomes more responsive to the needs of the movement, and in turn is able to supply them with the resources which can aid them in actualizing their cultural identity. In short, it consists of individuals in this country developing a cultural reciprocity. For example, I should not expect the Appalachian to have and develop the same values I have, unless he wants me to share these values with him. Similarly, he shouldn't expect me to accept his values. Yet, in a process of reciprocity we could learn from each other while actualizing our separate identities and culture. That is, the Appalachian may be able to show me how to be content with life without materialism or how to become more I-Thou oriented instead of my present I-It orientation. On the other hand, he may want to learn from me such things as community organization skills, flood and pollution control, lobby techniques, urban politics, etc. This type of relationship between us may make the West Virginia state motto, "Montani Semper Liberi," which means "Mountaineers Are Always Free," a reality for both of us.

> The bird fights its way out of the egg, the egg is the world, who would be born must first destroy the world.
>
> Herman Hesse